THE ANANDA COOKBOOK

The *Ananda* COOKBOOK

Easy-to-Prepare Recipes for the Vegetarian *Gourmet*

ANANDA PUBLICATIONS
14618 Tyler Foote Road   Nevada City, California 95959

Cover photograph by Wayne Green
Pictured left to right:
Nancy Mair, Asha Praver, Sheila Gilchrist

Poetry by J. Donald Walters

85 86 87 88 89 90   8 7 6 5 4 3 2

Copyright © 1985 by Ananda Publications

First printing 1985
International Standard Book Number 0-916124-26-6
Printed in the United States of America

Contents

The time has come for us to see
That there's but one reality
Upon the earth and high above
The truth that all was made from love.

Help us to find in every hour
In every thought, in every flower
A joy that spans eternity
The truth that makes us ever-free.

Ananda Cooperative Village

ANANDA COOPERATIVE VILLAGE, founded in 1967, is one of the best-known modern spiritual communities. Several hundred people live and work together in harmonious cooperation on 700 acres of land, developing spiritual models for marriage, childraising, interpersonal relationships, work, and the arts.

Joy will come to anyone
Whose soul has learned to fly!

Acknowledgements

THIS COOKBOOK is the product of many hands and hearts. We would like to thank all those who helped to create it, especially the many people at Ananda who shared their favorite recipes. Special thanks are due a number of people: Christine Ross and Nancy Mair for their dedication (and endurance!) in testing and retesting hundreds of recipes, and for their invaluable editorial assistance; Janice Boldt for the basic cover and page design; Julia Beinhorn, Martin Benkler, and Bella Potapovsky for their long hours of design work; Maria Potapovsky for typing hundreds of recipes; Dorothy Levit and Lynn Miller for typing the final manuscript; Patricia Black for her work on the index; George Beinhorn for his indispensable advice and assistance with tele-typesetting; Fern Lucki for helping to launch the project; David Praver for his support and confidence that the cookbook would indeed someday be ready; Garth Gilchrist and Joseph Okpaku for their patience and support; and J. Donald Walters for his guiding inspiration.

Asha Praver and Sheila Gilchrist
Cookbook Editors

YOU are the most important ingredient!

An Introduction

HAVE YOU EVER WONDERED why so many people claim that "Mom's cooking is best" and why, even if you follow her recipe, it just doesn't turn out the same? A good recipe is a starting point, but cooking well is more than a matter of technique. There are many intangibles which make the difference in how a meal tastes—your thoughts, your attitudes, your consciousness while you work. *You, in fact, are the most important ingredient in any recipe.* Food takes on the quality of the person preparing it, and if there is a special relationship between that person and the one being served—the food will show it. The old saying, "the way to a man's heart is through his stomach," contains more subtle truth than many people realize. Food, when prepared with love, satisfies more than the physical appetite. It nurtures on many levels.

Sound like a heavy responsibility? It really isn't. The best way to do it right is simply to have fun cooking. Just as your philodendron responds to your cheerful words and loving vibrations, so also do the carrots and the rice and the Italian salad dressing. They like to be treated kindly, with respect for what they have to offer. They will give more to you if you give more to them. Even if you are only slicing an apple—pay attention. Do it carefully, lovingly, as well as you can. Enjoy the process as well as the results and the results will be much more delicious.

A Note on Preparation Time

BY "PREPARATION TIME" we mean the time you are *actively* preparing the dish—sautéeing, chopping, stirring, blending, etc. Preparation time includes cooking time unless the dish cooks or bakes unattended for a long period, leaving you free to do other things. Where this is the case, we have listed cooking and preparation times separately.

Please note that all such times are averages which will vary from person to person, depending on experience.

Recipes

The world is waiting
  to tell you of a million things:
The shout of daybreak,
  The flutter of a robin's wings!
Come out and listen,
    There's magic for us all to share:
    For melody, melody's everywhere!

Soups

Leek Soup

Serves: 4-6

Preparation time: 40-45 minutes

Sauté in large saucepan over medium heat until tender:
6 tablespoons butter
5 medium leeks, minced (white part only)
1 medium-large onion, minced

Add, cover, and simmer for 15 minutes or until potatoes are tender:
4 cups vegetable broth (dissolve 4 unsalted vegetable bouillon cubes in 4 cups boiling water)
4 medium potatoes, cubed

Reserve 3 cups of soup and purée the rest in blender until smooth. Return to saucepan and add:
3 tablespoons chopped fresh chives
salt, to taste
½ teaspoon black pepper

Heat gently, stirring constantly until mixture comes to a boil. Serve at once.

Spinach-Herb Soup

Serves: 4-6

An excellent luncheon or first course dish.

Preparation time: 45-50 minutes

Sauté in heavy saucepan over medium heat until spinach and celery are wilted:

½ cup butter
4 rounded tablespoons chopped fresh chives
4 cups (packed) chopped fresh spinach, leaves only
    (about 2 large bunches)
2 cups finely chopped celery
2 teaspoons tarragon

Add:

6 cups water
8 salted vegetable bouillon cubes (Vegex brand tends
    to work best for this recipe)
1 teaspoon honey
¾ teaspoon garlic powder

Bring mixture to a boil, reduce heat, then simmer for 15 minutes. Purée mixture in blender until smooth. Serve garnished with any one or more of the following:

sour cream or yogurt
finely chopped fresh chives
slice of lemon
paprika

Bella's Borscht

Serves: 6-8

Preparation time: 30 minutes
Cooking time: 45 minutes

Place in large soup pot and bring to a boil:
   10 cups water
   4 cups diced beets
   4½ cups shredded cabbage
   2 cups sliced carrots
   3 cups chopped onions
   1½ cups diced potatoes
   1 small-medium bay leaf
   ¾ teaspoon garlic powder
   scant ½ teaspoon dried dill weed
   1 rounded teaspoon salt
   scant teaspoon black pepper

Reduce heat to simmer and cook covered for 45 minutes.
Serve with:
   dollop of sour cream and chopped chives

Cucumber-Yogurt Soup

Serves: 3-4

Preparation time: 15 minutes
Chilling time: 1 hour

Peel and grate:
2 large cucumbers

Blend in blender with grated cucumbers (in two batches):
4 cups yogurt
2 tablespoons olive oil
1½ tablespoons white wine vinegar
2 small garlic cloves, crushed
¾ teaspoon chopped fresh mint
⅛ teaspoon salt

Chill for 1 hour. Serve garnished with:
chopped fresh parsley

Oriental Miso Soup

Serves: 4-6

A fresh, full-bodied flavor.

Preparation time: 25 minutes

Bring to a boil, then simmer for 5 minutes:
  2 quarts water
  14 thin slices fresh ginger root (be sure to peel be-
    fore slicing)
  1 cup sliced mushrooms
  2 cups green peas, fresh or frozen
  ⅛ rounded teaspoon cayenne pepper
  ¼ rounded teaspoon cumin powder
  4 cloves garlic, minced or pressed
  1 large green onion, thinly sliced, including tops

Add:
  1¼ cups tomato juice

Remove from heat, cool slightly, then add, first mixing
with a little hot broth to liquify miso*:
  1 cup red miso

Remove ginger slices** and serve. Garnish with thinly
sliced tofu (optional).

Please note:

*Don't boil after adding miso. The high heat destroys
miso's living enzymes.

**If ginger slices sit in soup too long after adding miso,
the flavor will become too strong.

Hearty Miso-Onion Soup

Serves: 4

If you like French Onion Soup . . .

Preparation time: 25-30 minutes

Sauté in large saucepan over medium heat until onions are soft:
   6 tablespoons butter
   1½ large red onions, thinly sliced
   1½ cups (packed) sliced mushrooms

Add:
   3¾ cups water

Bring to a boil, then reduce heat. Stir in, first mixing with a little hot broth to liquify miso*:
   5-6 tablespoons red miso

Add:
   6 tablespoons freshly grated Parmesan cheese

Season with:
   3 tablespoons minced fresh parsley
   ⅛ teaspoon black pepper

Please note:
   *Don't boil after adding miso. The high heat destroys miso's living enzymes.

Gazpacho

Serves: 6-8

Refreshing and energizing. Lovely on a hot summer day.

Preparation time: 15 minutes
Chilling time: several hours

Combine in large bowl:
   1 large can (46 ounces) tomato juice
   2 cucumbers, peeled and diced
   2 green bell peppers, diced
   2 tomatoes, chopped
   5-6 tablespoons lemon juice (2 lemons)
   2 large cloves garlic, minced
   2 tablespoons finely chopped parsley or fresh
      coriander
   2 tablespoons olive oil
   ¼-½ teaspoon cumin powder
   salt, to taste
   ⅛-¼ teaspoon black pepper

Chill for several hours. Serve ice cold.

Tomato Soup

Serves: 4-6

Light and fresh-tasting.

Preparation time: 20-25 minutes
Cooking time: 1 hour

Sauté in large saucepan over medium heat:
3 tablespoons olive oil
1 large onion, chopped
1 large green bell pepper, chopped
3 cloves garlic, minced

Add:
3 cups tomato juice
3 cups peeled, seeded and chopped fresh tomatoes
1 salted vegetable bouillon cube
1½ teaspoons dried dill weed
1½ teaspoons basil
1 teaspoon dried parsley
⅛ teaspoon black pepper

Cover and cook over low heat for about 1 hour. Stir in:
1 teaspoon honey

Variation:
During last hour of cooking, add:
1 cup cubed raw potatoes

Cream of Cucumber Soup

Serves: 4-6

A delicate soup with a hint of curry.

Preparation time: 30 minutes

Melt in top of double boiler or over low heat:
  5 tablespoons butter

Add, whisk until thick, then remove from heat:
  6 tablespoons whole wheat pastry flour
  1¼ teaspoons salt
  3 cups milk

Sauté in skillet over medium heat for 2 minutes:

2 tablespoons butter
2 medium-large cucumbers, peeled, seeded and
   minced

Add and sauté until transparent:

1 medium onion, minced
½ teaspoon curry powder

Add, cover, and simmer for 5 minutes:

1 cup milk
2 cups water

Combine with hot white sauce and add:

¼ teaspoon freshly ground black pepper

Blend half of soup in blender until smooth. In a soup tureen, beat:

2 egg yolks

Slowly add unblended soup mixture to egg yolks, whisking as you pour. Then add the puréed soup and garnish with:

finely chopped chives or green onion tops

Serve hot or cold as a first course, or chilled as a light entrée. Served cold, garnish with:

dollop of unsweetened whipped cream and chopped
   chives

Cream of Broccoli-Leek Soup   Serves: 6-8

Preparation time: 35 minutes

In a large saucepan, sauté over medium heat for about 8 minutes:

1 cube butter (½ cup)
8 cups (packed) trimmed and coarsely chopped broccoli (approximately 2 pounds)
1½ cups sliced leeks (use white and light-green parts only)
1 medium-large potato, cubed

Add:

8 cups vegetable broth (dissolve 3 salted and 1 unsalted vegetable bouillon cubes in 8 cups boiling water)*

Bring to a boil, lower heat and cook for 15-20 minutes or until tender. Reserve ½ cup broccoli florets for garnish. Purée mixture in blender in batches until smooth. Return to saucepan and add:

black pepper, to taste

Heat through. Serve garnished with reserved broccoli. You might like to add:

dollop of sour cream sprinkled with paprika

Please note:

*For those who like very little salt, use 2 salted and 2 unsalted bouillon cubes, or if you like more salt, use 4 salted bouillon cubes.

Broccoli Bisque

Serves: 7-8

Very rich.

Preparation time: 30 minutes
Cooking time: 25 minutes

Sauté in large saucepan over medium heat until tender:
4 tablespoons butter
¾ cup thinly sliced yellow onions
¼ cup chopped green onions
1 cup sliced mushrooms

Add and stir until bubbling:
¼ cup whole wheat pastry flour

Remove from heat and gradually whisk in:
3 cups vegetable broth (dissolve 1½ salted vegetable bouillon cubes in 3 cups boiling water)

Return to heat and stir until thickened and smooth. Add:
1 cup broccoli florets (if large, split into smaller pieces)

Reduce heat and simmer for 20 minutes or until vegetables are tender. Add:
½ cup half and half
½ cup milk
2 cups grated Swiss cheese

Simmer until heated throughout and cheese is melted.

Variation:
For an extra-rich soup eliminate milk and use:
1 cup half and half

Potato-Cheese Soup

Serves: 4-6

A thick chowder-like soup.

Preparation time: 35 minutes

Boil until tender in large saucepan:

4 cups sliced potatoes
**4 cups vegetable broth (dissolve 1½-2 unsalted vege-
    table bouillon cubes in 4 cups boiling water)**
salt, to taste

Meanwhile, sauté until soft, then add to vegetable broth:

2 tablespoons butter
2 large celery stalks, finely chopped
1 medium onion, diced

Purée above ingredients in blender with:

1 tablespoon minced fresh parsley or more, to taste

Pour blended mixture into saucepan, reheat, and add:

3 cups milk
1 cup (packed) grated sharp cheddar cheese
1 teaspoon basil
½ teaspoon garlic powder
¼ teaspoon black pepper

Heat until cheese melts and flavors are well-blended—
about 5 to 10 minutes.

Czech Mushroom Soup

Serves: 6-8

Very rich.

Preparation time: 20 minutes
Cooking time: 20 minutes

Boil in large covered saucepan for 15 minutes:
4 cups water
4 medium-large potatoes*, diced
2 teaspoons salt
1 teaspoon caraway seeds

Reduce heat, mix together and stir into soup:
¼ cup whole wheat pastry flour
2 pints sour cream

Add and simmer (covered) for 10 minutes, stirring occasionally to prevent sticking:
1 pound sliced mushrooms

Remove from heat. Before serving, sprinkle with:
1 teaspoon dried dill weed or 1 tablespoon minced fresh dill

Variation:
For a less rich soup, use:
1 pint milk
1 pint sour cream

Please note:
*We prefer unpeeled potatoes. Peeled potatoes will give you a slightly smoother, more delicate flavor.

Deluxe Pea Soup with Curry   Serves: 6-8

Preparation time: 45 minutes
Cooking time: 1½ hours

Bring to a boil in large soup pot:
   10 cups water

Add, reduce heat, cover, and simmer for 1 hour:
   2½ cups green split peas
   6 unsalted vegetable bouillon cubes
   2 small onions, finely chopped
   4 large cloves garlic, minced
   2 large bay leaves
   salt, to taste

Meanwhile, sauté in medium skillet over medium heat
until almost tender:
   3 tablespoons butter
   2 large carrots, chopped
   1 small onion, chopped

After 1 hour, remove bay leaves from soup and press
soup through a sieve. Add carrot-onion mixture to soup,
simmer until carrots and onions are tender, then add:
   1½ teaspoons thyme
   1½ teaspoons marjoram
   1 teaspoon curry powder
   cayenne, to taste
   black pepper, to taste

Meanwhile, sauté in large skillet over medium heat until
soft:
   3 tablespoons butter
   ½ pound mushrooms, sliced

Add to sautéed mushrooms and cook until thickened:

2 tablespoons whole wheat pastry flour

Add a little of the soup to the mushroom mixture (roux) and whisk until smooth. Add thickened stock to rest of soup and heat through. Serve with:

dollop of sour cream or yogurt

Variation:

Add:

lemon juice, to taste
cubed cooked potatoes

Black Bean Soup

Serves: 6-8

Preparation time: 25 minutes
Cooking time: 2-2½ hours
Soaking time: overnight

Rinse, check for pebbles and discolored beans, then soak* overnight in large soup pot:

3 cups black beans
6 cups water

Drain the soaking water and refill soup pot with:

7 cups vegetable broth (dissolve 3½ unsalted vegetable bouillon cubes in 7 cups boiling water)

Add and cook for 2-2½ hours or until beans are soft:

1 large (28 ounce) can of tomatoes, including liquid (cut tomatoes into pieces)
2 cups chopped celery
1 large carrot, chopped
1 large onion, chopped
4 large cloves garlic, minced
2 bay leaves
1 teaspoon oregano
1 teaspoon basil
½ teaspoon marjoram

Add:

1½ tablespoons lemon juice
5½ tablespoons cooking sherry
apple cider vinegar, to taste (for a sharper flavor)
salt, to taste

Remove bay leaves and blend soup in food processor or blender. Return to soup pot**, reheat, and serve, garnishing each bowl with:

½-1 tablespoon sour cream
½ teaspoon chopped chives or green onion tops

Please note:

*Soaking beans helps you digest them more easily and shortens the cooking time.

**If you like a thinner soup, add a little more water at this point. Adjust seasonings, to taste.

Vegetable Soup with Lentils   Serves: 8-10

Preparation time: 25-30 minutes
Cooking time: 1 hour

Bring to a boil in large saucepan:

1 cup lentils
6 cups vegetable broth (dissolve 2½-3 salted
    vegetable bouillon cubes in 6 cups boiling water)

Add, reduce heat, cover, and simmer for 1 hour:

3 cups chopped fresh tomatoes
2 stalks celery, chopped
1 large potato, diced
1 large onion, chopped
1 large carrot, chopped
1 large green pepper, chopped
2 tablespoons fresh lemon juice
3 large cloves garlic, minced
2 bay leaves
¼ cup minced fresh parsley
½ teaspoon savory
½ teaspoon thyme
½ teaspoon oregano
salt and black pepper, to taste

Before serving, remove bay leaves and purée half of mixture in blender and add to rest of soup to thicken.

Give life your heart!
  Bless everything that's grown;
Fear not the loving:
  All this world's your own.

Salads

Greek Salad

Serves: 8-12

Colorful and festive.

Preparation time: 25 minutes

Line a large serving platter with red leaf or bibb lettuce leaves. In the center, mound:

½-¾ small head red cabbage, shredded

Encircle cabbage with:

1½ medium carrots, coarsely grated

Cube and place on top of the cabbage:

¾ pound feta cheese

Surround the cheese with:

1 pint whole Kalamata olives

Encircle the mound of carrots with 12 stacks, each consisting of:

1 tomato slice
1 red onion slice (⅛-inch thick)
1 green bell pepper ring (⅛-inch thick)
1 cucumber slice (⅛-inch thick)

Add and arrange decoratively along the outside of the ring:

one 14¾-ounce jar marinated artichoke hearts, drained
1 small cauliflower, broken into florets

Just before serving, sprinkle salad with:

olive oil
red wine vinegar
salt and black pepper, to taste

Garnish with:

fresh or dried basil

Rainbow Salad

Serves: 8-12

A meal in itself.

Preparation time: 45-50 minutes
Chilling time: overnight

Place in layers in large glass bowl:

2 medium heads iceberg lettuce, coarsely chopped
1 cup chopped green onions
one 8-ounce can water chestnuts, drained and sliced
1 small package frozen petite peas, thawed and un-
    cooked
½ cup freshly grated Parmesan cheese
1 cup chopped celery

Cover the above with mixture of:

1 cup mayonnaise
1 cup sour cream
1 cup herb salad dressing (page 61)

Chill overnight. Then add next three layers of:

5 hard-boiled eggs, chopped
enough tomato slices to cover top layer
1 cup vegetarian baco bits (optional)

Serve garnished with:

chopped ripe black olives

Great for picnics, parties, brunches, etc.

Raw Vegetable Salad

Serves: 2-4

Preparation time: 20 minutes

Combine in large bowl:
   1½ cups grated carrots
   1 tomato, chopped
   1 avocado, chopped
   ½ cup grated beets (peel large or tough-skinned beets
      before grating)
   2 tablespoons-¼ cup sunflower seeds

Mix together and pour over vegetables (you may not
want to use all of the dressing):
   ¾ cup light vegetable oil
   2 tablespoons red wine vinegar
   1 teaspoon tamari
   ¾ teaspoon nutritional yeast
   1¼ teaspoons molasses
   ⅛ teaspoon Vegit (available at health food stores)
   ⅛ teaspoon garlic powder
   ⅛ teaspoon onion powder

Serve on a bed of lettuce.

Jicama Salad

Serves 8

Preparation time: 25 minutes
Soaking time: 2 hours

Soak covered in slightly salted water for 2 hours:
1 medium red onion, thinly sliced into rounds

Blend together:
3 tablespoons fresh lemon juice or more, to taste
1½ tablespoons lime juice or more, to taste
1½ teaspoons grated lemon peel
pinch of salt
black pepper, to taste

Slowly whisk in:
6 tablespoons peanut oil
¾ cup olive oil
1 tablespoon minced fresh parsley

In a large bowl, place:
1½-1¾ pounds jicama, peeled and cut into matchstick julienne

Add vinaigrette to jicama and toss. Drain, pat dry, and stir in onion rings. On a platter, arrange:
red leaf lettuce leaves

Place jicama and onion on top of lettuce. Garnish with:
cherry tomatoes
green bell pepper rings

Serve immediately.

Cole Slaw

Serves: 6

Preparation time: 10-15 minutes
Chilling time: several hours

Mix together:

4 cups grated or shredded green cabbage
1 medium carrot, grated
½ cup mayonnaise
2 tablespoons lemon juice
scant tablespoon grated onion
½ teaspoon salt
⅛ teaspoon black pepper
1 tablespoon poppy seeds
1 teaspoon honey (optional)

This salad tastes best when refrigerated for several hours
to allow flavors to blend.

Variation:

Add:

½ cup finely chopped green bell pepper

For a more colorful salad, use purple cabbage.

Carrot Salad

Serves: 4

Preparation time: 10 minutes
Chilling time: 45 minutes

Mix together in large bowl:

3 cups shredded carrots (about 3 large carrots)
¼ cup raisins
1-1½ teaspoons lemon juice
1 tablespoon honey (add another ½ teaspoon if carrots aren't very sweet)
½ cup mayonnaise

Chill and serve.

Variations:

1. Instead of mayonnaise, use:

   ½ cup yogurt

   Omit lemon juice and add:

   2 tablespoons chopped cashews

2. For a more substantial salad, add to basic recipe:

   ½ cup grated Jack or cheddar cheese
   2 tablespoons chopped cashews

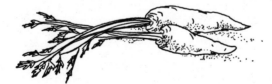

Tomato-Mushroom Salad with Marinade

Serves: 8

Preparation time: 25 minutes
Chilling time: several hours

To make marinade, blend in blender:

1¼ cups olive oil
2 tablespoons lemon juice
6 tablespoons red wine vinegar
4 large or 8 small cloves garlic
1½ teaspoons basil
¼ teaspoon black pepper
2 teaspoons chopped fresh parsley
1 tablespoon plus 1 teaspoon Worcestershire sauce
1 tablespoon plus 1 teaspoon dry mustard
1 teaspoon honey

Pour marinade over:

1 bunch green onions (about 7) including tops, sliced
    very thin
5 large tomatoes, cut into eighths (then sliced
    crossways if desired)
10 cups button mushrooms, quartered

Mix well and refrigerate for several hours. Stir
occasionally.

Beet Salad

Serves: 5-6

Light and flavorful.

Preparation time: 20 minutes
Cooking time: 20-25 minutes

In a large bowl, mix together:
⅓ cup mayonnaise
1 tablespoon lemon juice
scant teaspoon salt

Add:
4 cups diced cooked beets
2 tablespoons finely chopped chives or green onions
1 tablespoon chopped fresh parsley

Mix well and taste. Add more salt and/or lemon juice if needed. This dish keeps well in the refrigerator and can be prepared in advance.

French Vegetable Salad

Serves: 8-10

A decorative luncheon dish.

Preparation time: 30-35 minutes

Peel, cut into quarters, and steam until crisp-tender:
4 small beets (about 10 ounces)

Rinse cooked beets under cold water and pat dry. While beets are cooking, coarsely grate:
2 medium zucchini
2 medium carrots

Steam for several minutes until crisp-tender:
one 20-ounce package frozen French green beans

Line a serving platter with red leaf or bibb lettuce leaves. Mound green beans in center. Encircle the beans with grated carrots, then with zucchini. Add in whatever decorative pattern you choose:
1 basket cherry tomatoes
one 5¾-ounce can black olives, drained

Then add quartered beets. Garnish with:
raw sunflower seeds
chopped fresh chives

Serve with your favorite French dressing.

French Potato Salad

Serves: 8-10

A *tangy, marinated version.*

Preparation time: 30 minutes
Chilling time: 30 minutes

Boil in skins until done but not mushy:
10 large potatoes

While potatoes cook, blend in blender:
½ cup vegetable oil
½ cup apple cider vinegar
3 teaspoons salt
¾ teaspoon black pepper
1 tablespoon dry mustard
1½ teaspoons basil
1½ teaspoons thyme
1½ teaspoons dried dill weed or more, to taste
1½ teaspoons tarragon
2 large cloves garlic
1 tablespoon honey

Cut warm potatoes, peeled or unpeeled, into dressing.
Mix well and chill. Add:
**¼ cup minced green onions (including tops) or more,
    to taste**
1½ cups mayonnaise
chopped celery, to taste (optional)

Garnish as desired with any one or more of the following:
black or pimiento-stuffed green olives
parsley
chopped chives

Hot German Potato Salad

Preparation time: 35-40 minutes

Boil in skins until done:
7 medium-large potatoes cut in fourths, lengthwise

Meanwhile, cook according to package instructions:
one 5-ounce package stripples

Remove stripples from skillet with slotted spoon and drain on a paper towel. Sauté in same skillet using leftover oil until onions are transparent:
1¼ cups chopped onions
½ teaspoon caraway seeds
¾ cup chopped celery
1½ teaspoons dill weed
1 teaspoon crushed tarragon

Add crumbled cooked stripples. In a separate skillet, bring to a boil and add to sautéed mixture:
2 teaspoons honey
⅜ cup water
¾ cup apple cider vinegar or more, to taste
¼ teaspoon paprika
½ teaspoon dry mustard

Dice the cooked potatoes and add to the sautéed mixture. Add:
salt and pepper, to taste

Serve with:
chopped fresh parsley or chives

Country-Style Potato Salad

Serves: 4

Preparation time: 15 minutes
Cooking time: 20-30 minutes
Chilling time: 30 minutes

Boil until tender:
4 large white potatoes, diced

Meanwhile, hard boil:
2 eggs

While potatoes are still warm add and mix well:
1 tablespoon apple cider vinegar
½ teaspoon garlic powder
⅛-¼ teaspoon salt
¼ teaspoon beau monde or celery salt
¼ cup minced red or yellow onions
pinch of dry mustard

Let cool. Add and mix well:
1 tablespoon light vegetable oil
¼ cup plus 2 tablespoons mayonnaise
2 hard-boiled eggs, chopped

Sprinkle lightly with:
paprika

Variation:
For a slightly different taste, add:
¼ teaspoon dried dill weed
¼ cup chopped celery

Mexican Salad

Serves: 6

A meal in itself—one of our favorites.

Preparation time: 25 minutes
Cooking time for rice: 45 minutes
Chilling time: 30 minutes

Sauté for 5 minutes in medium skillet:
1½ tablespoons butter
1½ cups cooked rice
scant ½ teaspoon chile powder
⅛ teaspoon coriander
scant ½ teaspoon cumin powder
½ teaspoon garlic powder
¼ teaspoon paprika

Allow to cool. In a large bowl, mix the above with:
1½ cups cooked kidney beans (canned work fine)
1 head iceberg lettuce, cut into bite-size pieces
¼-½ cup minced yellow or red onions
one 4-ounce can diced Ortega chiles
one 3½-5-ounce can pitted black olives, sliced

Then add:
3 tomatoes, diced
⅓ pound cheddar cheese, cut into small pieces

Top with:
¼ pound corn chips, broken into bite-size pieces

Chill and serve with Ranch Dressing (page 57). This
salad goes well with corn bread.

Macaroni Salad

Serves: 6-8

Preparation time: 40-45 minutes

Bring to a boil and cook in salted water (be careful not to overcook):

6 cups sesame or vegetable macaroni (vegetable makes a colorful salad)

Rinse with cold water and drain. Combine cooked macaroni with:

2 cups finely chopped celery
½-¾ cup finely chopped red onions
1¼ cups mayonnaise
5 tablespoons garlic red wine vinegar
one 10-ounce package frozen peas, cooked and drained
2 cups cooked kidney beans
½ teaspoon dry mustard or, to taste
1 rounded teaspoon basil
1 teaspoon garlic powder
1 teaspoon Spike (available at health food stores)
salt and black pepper, to taste
1 large can black olives, sliced
chopped green pepper, to taste

Sprinkle with:

chopped fresh parsley

Variation:

Add:

5 hard-boiled eggs, chopped
cubed cheese

Tabouli

Serves: 6-7

Preparation time: little over 1 hour
Soaking time: 1 hour
Chilling time: 1 hour

Combine, cover and soak for 1 hour:
   4½ cups boiling water
   2¼ cups dry bulgur wheat

Meanwhile, combine in large bowl:
   1½ cups lemon juice
   1 tablespoon dried mint, or fresh mint, to taste
   1½ teaspoons garlic powder
   2 teaspoons salt
   1 teaspoon black pepper

Whisk in slowly:
   1⅛ cups safflower oil

Stir in:
   2¼ cups (packed) finely chopped parsley (about 4
      large bunches)
   ¾ cup chopped green onions (including tops)
   3 tomatoes, finely diced

Mix together with soaked wheat and refrigerate for
1 hour or, even better, overnight. Goes well with
Marinated Tofu (page 233).

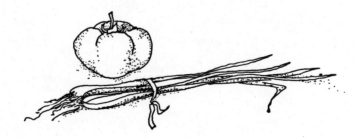

Summer Rice Salad

Serves: 6-8

Preparation time: 50 minutes (not including time for cooking rice)
Chilling time: 1 hour

Combine in large bowl:

    6 cups warm brown rice (you can use warmed
        leftover rice or freshly cooked rice)
    two 6-ounce jars marinated artichoke hearts,
        chopped, including marinade
    4 tablespoons red wine vinegar
    3 tablespoons lemon juice
    4 tablespoons olive oil
    1½ teaspoons thyme or more, to taste
    1¼ teaspoons garlic powder or more, to taste
    2½ teaspoons basil
    salt and black pepper, to taste
    one 3-ounce jar pimiento-stuffed green olives,
        drained and sliced
    one large (about 6 ounces) can pitted black olives,
        drained and sliced

Chill the above. While mixture chills, prepare:

    1 cup chopped green bell peppers
    2 cups peeled, seeded, and chopped cucumbers
    6 large green onions, chopped (tops included)
    4 large tomatoes, chopped
    ¾ cup finely chopped fresh parsley
    1½ cups chopped celery

After salad chills stir in an additional:

    4 tablespoons red wine vinegar
    3 tablespoons olive oil

Adjust seasoning if necessary. Serve on a bed of lettuce
leaves garnished with:

    cherry tomatoes
    green bell pepper rings
    olives

Egg Salad

Serves: 2-3

Preparation time: 20 minutes

Coarsely chop:
6 hard-boiled eggs

Combine with eggs in large bowl and mix well:
3 tablespoons mayonnaise
¼ rounded teaspoon curry powder
¼ teaspoon cumin powder
⅛ teaspoon Spike (available at health food stores)
¼ teaspoon grey Poupon mustard
black pepper, to taste
2 tablespoons minced celery
salt, to taste

Egg Salad with Cashews

Serves: 3-4

Preparation time: 20 minutes

Coarsely chop:
1 dozen hard-boiled eggs

Combine with eggs in large bowl and mix well:
2 tablespoons wet mustard or more, to taste
½ cup plus 2 tablespoons mayonnaise
salt and black pepper, to taste
¼ teaspoon paprika
2 tablespoons minced fresh chives
½ cup finely chopped toasted cashews or more, to taste

Garnish with any of the following:
  sliced avocado
  sliced mushrooms
  sprouts

Tofu Salad

Serves: 4

"Mock tuna salad".

Preparation time: 15 minutes

Mix together in large bowl:
  1 pound tofu, drained, rinsed, and mashed
  ½ cup mayonnaise
  4 tablespoons catsup
  2-3 tablespoons tamari or, to taste
  4 tablespoons nutritional yeast
  1½-2 cups chopped celery
  ¼ teaspoon herb salt or Spike (available in health
    food stores)
  1 teaspoon onion powder
  ½ teaspoon garlic powder

Serve with vegetable sticks, chips, or as a sandwich
spread.

Variations:
  1. For a spicier version add:
    ½ cup Picante sauce or more, to taste

  2. Add to salad and adjust seasonings:
    cooked elbow macaroni
    mayonnaise

Apple-Celery Salad
with Banana Dressing

Serves: 3-5

Preparation time: 15 minutes

Combine in medium bowl and set aside:
¼-⅓ cup chopped dates (4 large dates)
½ cup chopped celery (1-2 stalks)
2 large or 4 small diced green apples

Grind in blender:
¼ cup walnuts

Then add:
2 ripe mashed bananas
1 tablespoon honey
1 tablespoon freshly squeezed lemon juice

Combine banana mixture with apples and celery. Top servings with:
⅓ cup chopped walnuts

Serve immediately. The banana dressing darkens quickly, although it will still taste fine.

Variation:
Instead of dates, use:
2 tablespoons raisins

Festive Cranberry Salad

Serves: 6-8

Preparation time: 20 minutes
Chilling time: 1-1½ hours

Boil in saucepan until skins pop:
   12 ounces fresh cranberries
   1 cup water

Add and let cool a bit:
   ½-¾ cup honey

Pour cranberry mixture into large bowl. Add and mix well:
   1 cup grated coconut
   4 oranges, peeled, seeded, sectioned and diced
   ½ cup chopped walnuts

Chill and serve.

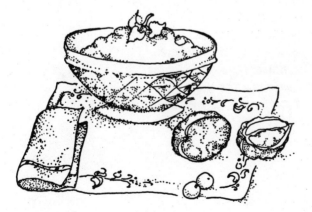

There's joy in the heavens,
A smile on the mountains,
  And melody sings everywhere.
    The flowers are all laughing
    To welcome the morning;
      Your soul is as free as the air.

Salad Dressings

Tomato Juice
Salad Dressing

Makes: 1½ cups

Preparation time: 5-10 minutes

Blend in blender:
 1 cup thick tomato juice
 4 tablespoons safflower oil
 4 tablespoons apple cider vinegar
 ½ teaspoon basil
 3 cloves garlic
 ⅛ teaspoon freshly ground black pepper
 honey, to taste

Tangy Tomato Dressing

Makes: 1½ cups

Preparation time: 5 minutes

Blend in blender:
 ⅔ cup vegetable oil
 ⅓ cup catsup
 1½ tablespoons honey or more, to taste
 ⅓ cup red wine vinegar (we recommend
  garlic-flavored)
 2 teaspoons Worcestershire sauce

Toss salad with dressing. Add:
 salt and black pepper, to taste

Goes well with a spinach-raw mushroom salad.

Ranch Dressing

Makes: 2 cups

Preparation time: 10 minutes

Mix together or blend in blender:
   1 cup mayonnaise
   1 cup buttermilk
   1 tablespoon plus 1 teaspoon chopped chives or finely
      chopped green onions (tops only)
   2 teaspoons parsley
   ¼ rounded teaspoon garlic powder
   ¼ teaspoon cumin powder
   ¼ rounded teaspoon onion powder
   small pinch of cayenne
   dash of paprika
   generous pinch of salt
   generous pinch of black pepper

Refrigerate 1 hour or longer to allow flavors to blend (optional).

Blue Cheese Dressing

Makes: 1½ cups

Preparation time: 5-10 minutes

Mix together or blend in blender:
   ½ cup sour cream
   ½ cup mayonnaise
   ¼ cup buttermilk
   ¼ teaspoon garlic powder
   ⅛ teaspoon onion powder
   1-3 tablespoons blue cheese
   pinch of cayenne

Creamy Italian Dressing

Makes: 2 cups

Preparation time: 5-8 minutes

Blend in blender:
  ⅓ cup water
  ¼ cup apple cider vinegar
  1 tablespoon honey
  1 egg
  ½ teaspoon celery seed
  ⅛ teaspoon dry mustard
  1 large clove garlic
  1 teaspoon savory
  1 teaspoon tarragon
  1 teaspoon salt
  ½ teaspoon black pepper

While blender is on, slowly add:
  1 cup vegetable oil

Yogurt Salad Dressing

Makes: 2 cups

Preparation time: 5-8 minutes

Combine and mix well:
  2 cups yogurt (thinned with milk if desired)
  ¾ teaspoon garlic powder
  ½ teaspoon onion powder
  ¾ teaspoon dried dill weed
  ¼ teaspoon beau monde or celery salt
  ¼ teaspoon paprika
  ½ teaspoon cumin powder
  ¼ teaspoon salt

Variations:

> Blend above mixture in blender with any of the following:
>
> > ½ cup chopped cooked beets (do not thin yogurt)
> > chopped fresh tomatoes, to taste (do not thin yogurt)
> > mashed avocado, to taste

Cassidy French Dressing   Makes: 1½ cups

Preparation time: 10 minutes

Blend in blender:
  ¼-⅓ cup apple cider vinegar
  2 tablespoons Dijon prepared mustard
  1 tablespoon honey
  ½ teaspoon salt

Slowly add and blend with rest of mixture:
  1 cup olive oil

Add to above mixture:
  2 cloves garlic, minced
  2 tablespoons chopped yellow or red onions
  ¼ cup finely chopped fresh parsley (remove stems)

Refrigerate for 1 hour to allow flavors to blend (optional).

Luscious Green Dressing
Makes: 2 cups

Slightly sweet yet tangy.

Preparation time: 10 minutes

Blend in blender:
    1 cup safflower or olive oil
    ½ cup apple cider vinegar
    1 cup chopped fresh parsley (remove stems)
    1 small green onion, chopped
    2 tablespoons peeled and grated ginger root
    ⅓ cup honey
    ⅛ teaspoon basil
    ¼ rounded teaspoon curry powder
    ¼ teaspoon dry mustard
    ⅛ teaspoon salt
    pinch of black pepper

Herb Salad Dressing

Makes: 2¼ cups

Rich, pungent taste.

Preparation time: 5 minutes

Blend in blender:
  1¼ cups vegetable oil
  ⅓-½ cup apple cider vinegar
  ¼ cup lemon juice
  1 tablespoon tamari
  1 teaspoon garlic powder
  ½ teaspoon oregano
  ¼ teaspoon marjoram
  ¼ teaspoon tarragon
  ¼ teaspoon rosemary
  2 tablespoons finely grated Parmesan cheese
  ¼ cup sesame seeds, lightly toasted*
  ½ teaspoon dry mustard (optional—for a sharper
    taste)

Please note:
  *To toast sesame seeds:

Place a skillet over medium heat. Add sesame seeds. Stir frequently for several minutes until seeds begin popping and turn *slightly* darker in color. Be careful—they burn quickly.

Lemon-Cucumber Dressing

Makes: 1 quart

Lemony-sweet dressing with a hint of dill.

Preparation time: 12-15 minutes

Blend in blender:
1 cup fresh lemon juice
½ cup oil (preferably olive or sesame)
3 large cucumbers, peeled and coarsely chopped
3 tablespoons honey
4¼ teaspoons tamari
¾ teaspoon dried dill or more, to taste
½ teaspoon garlic powder or more, to taste

While blending, add:
¾ cup sunflower seeds

Lemon- Parsley Salad Dressing

Makes: 3 cups

Preparation time: 15 minutes

Blend in blender:
1 cup vegetable oil
4 teaspoons apple cider vinegar
½ cup lemon juice
2 cups (packed) fresh parsley
½ teaspoon marjoram
⅓ cup chopped green bell pepper
1 teaspoon salt
dash black pepper

Lemon-Tahini Dressing

Makes: 2 cups

A light, airy tahini dressing.

Preparation time: 20 minutes

In a blender, combine:
½ cup olive oil
4 tablespoons lemon juice

Add and blend:
1 large clove garlic
3 tablespoons minced onion
2 stalks celery with leaves, chopped
2 tablespoons chopped fresh parsley
⅛ teaspoon salt

Add and blend:
½ cup sesame tahini

Tahini Dressing

Makes: 1½ cups

Good with salads. Wonderful on sesame-tofu burgers (page 119).

Preparation time: 10 minutes

Blend in blender:
- ½ cup water
- ½ cup tahini
- 2 tablespoons tamari (use ¼ cup for dressing for burgers)
- ¼ cup apple cider vinegar
- ½ teaspoon garlic powder
- ½ teaspoon dried dill weed
- ¼ cup barley malt syrup
- ¼ cup sesame seeds
- ½ teaspoon mixed herb seasoning (we recommend Vegit, which can be found in most health food stores)

Add water to thin if necessary. This dressing is thick and pungent. Those who like the flavor of tahini will enjoy it.

Tamari Salad Dressing

Makes: 2 cups

Surprisingly good!

Preparation time: 5-8 minutes

Blend in blender:
- 1 cup safflower oil
- ½ cup apple cider vinegar
- ¼ cup tamari
- ¼ cup honey

Variations:

    Add any one or more of the following:

        ¼ **cup nutritional yeast or more, to taste**
        herbal seasoning, to taste
        1 teaspoon basil or, to taste

Poppy Seed Dressing

Makes: 2½-3 cups

Sweet and creamy.

Preparation time: 10 minutes

    Blend in blender:

        ½ **cup water**
        ½ **cup honey or, to taste**
        ¼ **cup apple cider vinegar**
        2 tablespoons prepared mustard
        3 rounded tablespoons chopped onions
        1 tablespoon poppy seeds
        1 teaspoon salt

    Slowly add and blend with rest of mixture:

        1½ **cups safflower or sesame oil**

This dressing is especially good on spinach salad.

Tropical Blend
Fruit Salad Dressing

Makes: 2½-3 cups

Preparation time: 10-15 minutes

Combine in blender until smooth:
   1½ cups cream
   1 cup ripe mango pulp
   ½ tablespoon minced fresh mint
   2 tablespoons honey, to taste
   ¼ cup ground almonds

Orange-Cream
Fruit Salad Dressing

Makes: 3 cups

Preparation time: 10 minutes

Combine in blender until smooth:
 1½ cups cream
 ½ cup freshly squeezed orange juice
 ½ avocado or 1 banana
 2 tablespoons honey or, to taste
 ½ cup chopped dates, raisins, or currants

Avocado-Orange
Fruit Salad Dressing

Makes: 1-2 cups

Preparation time: 10 minutes

Combine in blender until smooth:
 juice of 3-4 medium oranges (depending on how
   thick you like your dressing)
 1 avocado
 2 small bananas (or 1 large)
 ½ cup ground almonds

Leave home in the sunshine:
Dance through a meadow—
   Or sit by a stream and just be.
The lilt of the water
Will gather your worries
   And carry them down to the sea.

*Vegetables,
Side Dishes*

Lemon-Herb Cauliflower

Serves: 8

Preparation time: 20-25 minutes
Baking time: 15-20 minutes

Preheat oven to 375°. Break into florets and steam until crisp-tender:

2 large heads cauliflower (about 5 pounds)

While the above cooks, sauté for several minutes:

1 cube butter (½ cup)
3 large cloves garlic, pressed

Add:

¾ teaspoon basil
¾ teaspoon oregano
salt and black pepper, to taste
5 tablespoons fresh lemon juice or more, to taste

Arrange cauliflower in a 2½-quart baking dish. Add butter mixture and stir well. Sprinkle with:

1 cup finely grated fresh Parmesan cheese
paprika

Bake at 375° for 15-20 minutes until golden brown and cheese is melted.

Italian Green Beans

Serves: 5-6

Preparation time: 25-30 minutes

Cook in boiling salted water until crisp-tender:
2 pounds frozen Italian green beans

While the above cooks, sauté until golden:
¼ cup olive oil
2 tablespoons butter
4 large cloves garlic, minced
1 medium-large onion, chopped

Drain beans and add to onions and garlic along with:
½ cup minced fresh parsley
3 tablespoons fresh lemon juice
1½ teaspoons marjoram
salt and black pepper, to taste

Cook until beans are heated through and serve.

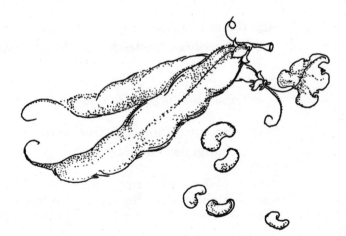

Turnips au Gratin

Serves: 6-7

Preparation time: 30-35 minutes
Baking time: 15-20 minutes

Preheat oven to 350°. Steam until crisp-tender:

**5-6 large turnips (about 3 pounds), peeled and sliced
¼-inch thick**

While turnips are cooking, sauté until golden:

**¼ cup butter
⅓ cup minced fresh parsley
4 medium garlic cloves, minced**

Remove from heat, add steamed turnips, mix thoroughly
and add:

salt and black pepper, to taste

Rub an 8-inch square baking dish with the cut side of a
peeled garlic clove, cut in half. Arrange turnips and
butter in dish. Scald:

**1 cup half and half
1 cup milk**

Add to hot milk and whisk until smooth and thick:

2 tablespoons cornstarch (dissolved in a little milk)

Add:

salt and black pepper, to taste

Pour sauce over turnips. Sprinkle with:

1½ cups grated Gruyère cheese

Bake at 350° for 15 minutes, then put under broiler for
several minutes until cheese is golden brown. Watch
closely so cheese does not burn. Pour off excess oil if
desired.

Herbed Carrots

Serves: 6

Preparation time: 45-50 minutes

Sauté until golden:
4 tablespoons butter
3 tablespoons olive oil
3 tablespoons minced onion
2 large cloves garlic, minced

Add and cook for 5 more minutes:
2 pounds carrots, sliced into thin rounds

Add, stir, cover, and cook for 10 more minutes:
2 teaspoons honey
2 bay leaves
1 cup dry white wine

Add:
4 tablespoons chopped fresh parsley
1 tablespoon basil
salt and black pepper, to taste
freshly grated nutmeg, to taste

Increase heat to medium-high and cook uncovered until carrots are crisp-tender and liquid has evaporated.
Remove bay leaves and serve.

Spicy Zucchini and Cabbage   Serves: 4

Preparation time: 25 minutes

Sauté in large skillet (covered) over high heat until crisp-tender:

5 tablespoons butter
a few drops sesame oil
¾ large cabbage, shredded (about 6 cups)
1 medium onion, thinly sliced (about 2 cups)

Add, cover, and cook until zucchini are tender:

3 medium zucchini, sliced (about 3 cups)
¼ rounded teaspoon crushed red pepper flakes

Then add:

½ teaspoon salt
black pepper, to taste
1½ tablespoons tamari or more, to taste

Sprinkle with:

¼-⅓ cup toasted sesame seeds

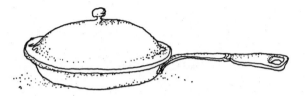

Cumin Sweet Potatoes

Serves: 5-6

A spicy, aromatic blend of Middle-Eastern flavors.

Preparation time: 25-30 minutes

Sauté in large skillet over medium heat for 15 minutes:
4-6 tablespoons butter
2 large onions, cut into chunks
**2 pounds sweet potatoes (slender if possible), peeled
and cut into ¼-inch slices**

Add and cook until cumin seed has browned and
vegetables are tender:
3 large green bell peppers, cut into chunks
2½ tablespoons cumin seed (not powder)
salt or tamari, to taste

Please note:
You may steam sweet potatoes until crisp-tender instead
of sautéeing them, but be careful not to overcook.

Sweet and Sour Vegetables   Serves: 6-8

Very colorful.

Preparation time: 45 minutes

In a large saucepan, bring to a boil and cook until thickened:

⅛ cup tomato purée
¼ cup soy sauce
⅓ cup honey
¼ cup cooking sherry
1½ tablespoons cornstarch (dissolved in pineapple juice)
⅓ cup unsweetened pineapple juice

While the sauce is cooking, cover and steam until almost crisp-tender:

2 cups sliced carrots

Then turn off heat, add, cover, and cook until crisp-tender:

2 cups chopped bok choy (the heat from the pan will cook bok choy)

Add steamed carrots and bok choy to the sauce. Then add:

1 cup chopped onions
2 cups chopped green peppers
2 cups chopped unsweetened pineapple
1 small can drained sliced water chestnuts
3 cups chopped tomatoes

Simmer together until vegetables are tender but still somewhat crisp. Then add:

¼ cup unsweetened pineapple juice
1½-2 tablespoons cornstarch (dissolved in pineapple juice, as above)

Cook until thickened. Serve with rice or noodles.

Variation:

Use mixture as a filling for crêpes. Sprinkle crêpes with sesame seeds.

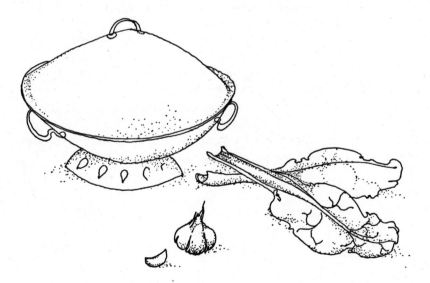

Sautéed Spinach
Oriental Style

Serves: 4-6

Preparation time: 30-40 minutes

Sauté over high heat in large skillet, stirring often, until spinach is tender and liquid is almost evaporated:

3 tablespoons butter
½ teaspoon sesame oil or more, to taste
3 pounds fresh spinach, coarsely chopped (leaves only)
3 tablespoons tamari or more, to taste
½ tablespoon honey
2 tablespoons mirin (sweet cooking sake) or dry sherry

Remove spinach with slotted spoon and form a mound in the center of a large serving platter. Add to skillet and sauté about 3 minutes, stirring often, until crisp-tender:

2 tablespoons tamari or more, to taste
½ teaspoon sesame oil or more, to taste
12 ounces mung sprouts

Remove sprouts with slotted spoon and arrange in a circle around spinach. Sauté until warmed through in the remaining oil-tamari mixture:

one 8-ounce can water chestnuts, drained and sliced

Garnish spinach with water chestnuts. Sprinkle over top:

1 tablespoon toasted sesame seeds

Burnt Eggplant

Serves: 6

A traditional Indian side dish.
The burnt flavor is part of its uniqueness.

Preparation time: 50-55 minutes

How to "burn" an eggplant: Cook eggplant over an open flame by placing it directly on gas burner. Rotate eggplant to char all sides evenly. Eggplant will gradually collapse as flesh becomes soft.

Burn and set aside to cool:

5 medium-large eggplants

Sauté in large skillet or saucepan over medium-low heat until garlic and onions are transparent:

½ cup butter
2 large cloves garlic, pressed, or more, to taste
½ large onion, finely grated (including juice)
1½ teaspoons salt or more, to taste
¼ yellow chile, minced (use more for a hotter version)

Spoon cooled insides of eggplants into the sauce and mix well. Bring the mixture to a boil so that the sauce saturates the eggplant.

Scalloped Corn

Serves: 8

Preparation time: 15 minutes
Baking time: 1 hour 20 minutes

Preheat oven to 325°. Butter a deep 2½-quart baking dish. Combine the following ingredients and pour into dish:

3¼ cups fresh or frozen corn
5 eggs, beaten
2¾ cups half and half or cream
5 tablespoons butter, melted
3 tablespoons whole wheat pastry flour
3 tablespoons honey
¼ cup finely chopped onion
½ cup finely chopped green bell pepper
1½ teaspoons salt
¼ teaspoon black pepper
¼ teaspoon paprika

Bake at 325° for 20 minutes, then stir through. Continue baking for 1 hour until pudding is golden brown and a knife inserted in the center comes out clean.

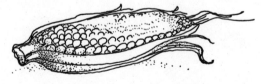

Herbed Millet

Serves: 3-4

Preparation time: 20 minutes
Cooking time: 30 minutes

Sauté in saucepan until onions are transparent:

4 tablespoons vegetable oil
½ large or 1 small onion, minced
2 cloves garlic, minced

Add:

½ teaspoon thyme
½ teaspoon basil
1½ teaspoons minced fresh parsley
½ teaspoon tarragon
½ teaspoon herb seasoning (Vegit or Spike)
⅛ teaspoon salt (eliminate if salted vegetable bouillon cube is used)
pinch of black pepper

Stir in:

1 cup raw millet

After stirring a few minutes, add:

2 cups boiling water
1 Huegli vegetable bouillon cube

Cover and simmer for 30 minutes.

Sesame Rice

Serves: 4-6

Preparation time: 25 minutes
Cooking time: 1 hour

Bring to a boil:

3 cups water

Add and once again bring to a boil:

1½ cups short grain brown rice

Reduce heat, cover, and simmer until liquid is absorbed (35-45 minutes). While rice cooks, sauté until golden brown, stirring frequently:

1 tablespoon butter
2 tablespoons chopped cashews

Remove and set aside. Heat:

3 tablespoons butter

Add and fry until seeds are golden brown, stirring frequently:

½ cup sesame seeds
¼ teaspoon cayenne or more, to taste
1 bay leaf, crumbled

Combine cashews and sesame seeds and stir into hot cooked rice. Add:

½ teaspoon salt or, to taste

Mix thoroughly. Sprinkle with:

juice of ½ lime
1 tablespoon rose water (optional)

Lemon Rice

Serves: 4

Preparation time: 10-15 minutes
Cooking time: 50-65 minutes

Bring to a boil:
   3 cups water

Add and once again bring to a boil:
   1½ cups brown rice

Reduce heat to simmer and simmer until liquid is absorbed (35-45 minutes). While rice cooks, lightly sauté in large skillet over medium heat until mustard seeds start to pop:
   4 tablespoons butter (half a cube)
   1 teaspoon black mustard seeds
   pinch-⅛ teaspoon cayenne
   2 teaspoons turmeric
   1 bay leaf, crumbled
   ½ teaspoon salt (if cooked rice is unsalted)

Add cooked rice and mix well. Then add:
   2 tablespoons freshly squeezed lemon juice

Cook until rice is warmed throughout.

Variations:
   Along with the rice, add any one or all of the following:
   2 tablespoons raisins
   ½-¾ cup cooked peas
   ½ cup sautéed onions (while rice is cooking, sauté onions until golden brown in 1-2 tablespoons butter)

Wild Rice-Chestnut Stuffing   Serves: 10

Preparation time: 40 minutes
Cooking time: 1 hour

Sauté in large saucepan until golden and soft:

6 tablespoons butter
12 ounces shallots, coarsely chopped

Add:

**1½ cups vegetable stock (6 unsalted vegetable
    bouillon cubes dissolved in 1½ cups boiling
    water)**
8 ounces wild rice
1¼ cups dry white wine
¾ cup minced fresh parsley
1 teaspoon salt
¾-1 teaspoon black pepper
2 teaspoons basil
1 teaspoon sage
¾ teaspoon thyme

Bring to a boil, then reduce heat to lowest setting and
cook covered until liquid is almost absorbed—about 50
minutes. When rice is almost done, sauté in skillet over
high heat until soft and liquid has evaporated:

4 tablespoons butter
1 pound mushrooms, sliced
1 cup chopped celery

Add mushroom mixture to cooked rice, then stir in and
cook for an additional 5-10 minutes or until all liquid is
absorbed:

**two 15½-ounce cans chestnuts, rinsed, drained and
    chopped**

Please note:

If fresh chestnuts are available, use 1-1¼ pounds,
blanched, peeled and coarsely chopped.

Breaded Mushrooms

Serves: 4

Preparation time: 40 minutes

Combine:

½ cup whole wheat pastry flour
½ teaspoon salt
¼ teaspoon black pepper

Combine in a separate bowl:

3 large egg yolks, beaten
1 tablespoon water
½ teaspoon salt
½ teaspoon garlic powder
¼ teaspoon black pepper
pinch of cayenne

Crumble:

3 slices toasted whole wheat bread

Wash, pat dry, and trim stalks of:

½ pound large mushrooms

Coat mushrooms with flour mixture. Then dip coated
mushrooms into egg yolk mixture. Roll mushrooms in
bread crumbs, completely covering them. Melt in skillet:

¼ cup butter
¼ cup vegetable oil

Fry mushrooms over medium heat until golden brown on
each side and tender when pierced with a fork. Watch
closely. They burn easily. After both sides are browned
you can cover skillet with a lid to speed up cooking time.

Serving suggestions:

Sprinkle with freshly grated Parmesan cheese or serve
with a dip or sauce.

Sing when the sun shines, sing when the rain falls,
  Sing when your road seems strange.
In a tempest seize the lightning flash
  And ride the winds of change!

Main Dishes

Broccoli-Noodle
Casserole with Cheese

Serves: 3-4

Preparation time: 30 minutes
Baking time: 20 minutes

Preheat oven to 400°. Bring to a boil:

8 cups water

Add to boiling water and cook until almost tender:

2 cups elbow macaroni
1 teaspoon oil
dash of salt

Drain noodles, rinse with cold water, and place in large casserole dish. While macaroni cooks, sauté until golden in medium-large skillet:

2 tablespoons butter
1 medium onion, chopped
1 clove garlic, minced
1 teaspoon dried parsley
pinch black pepper
3 tablespoons tamari
½ teaspoon paprika

Add and sauté (covered) until tender:

1 zucchini, sliced
2 cups chopped broccoli
1 medium tomato, chopped

Spoon sautéed vegetables over macaroni. Add and mix well:

1½ cups grated cheddar cheese

Sprinkle over top:

¼-½ cup fresh whole wheat bread crumbs

Bake at 400° for 20 minutes.

Broccoli Neapolitan

Serves: 6

Preparation time: 30 minutes

Cook until tender:

**2 bunches fresh broccoli (about 2 pounds or two
10-ounce packages frozen broccoli spears)**

Drain broccoli and set aside. Keep warm. While above
cooks, sauté in medium saucepan until golden:

**2 tablespoons olive oil
2 tablespoons butter
1 small onion, thinly sliced
2 large cloves garlic, minced**

Add to sautéed mixture and stir well:

3½ tablespoons whole wheat pastry flour

Stir in and cook over low heat until mixture is bubbly
and thick:

**1½ cups vegetable broth (use 1 unsalted vegetable
bouillon cube dissolved in 1½ cups boiling water)**

Add and cook until cheese melts:

**2 cups (packed) grated Jack cheese
½ teaspoon black pepper
½ cup sliced black olives
salt, to taste**

Arrange broccoli in a pie dish or shallow casserole. Pour
sauce over broccoli. Garnish with:

cherry tomatoes

Vegetable Roast

Serves: 4-6

Smells heavenly while baking.

Preparation time: 10-15 minutes
Baking time: 1½-2 hours

Preheat oven to 375°. Scrub and cut into large chunks:
   3 medium parsnips
   2 medium carrots
   6 medium turnips
   3 large potatoes

Place vegetables in large casserole dish, add, and stir:
   ½-¾ cup water
   2 tablespoons tamari
   6 tablespoons butter
   ¼ cup fresh minced parsley
   1½ teaspoons garlic powder

Cover and bake at 375° for 1½-2 hours. Yogurt-Cheese Sauce (page 151) goes well with this dish.

Deep Dish
Russian Vegetable Pie

Serves: 4-5

Preparation time: 60 minutes
Baking time: 35 minutes

Preheat·oven to 400°. To make pastry, double pie crust recipe (page 190). Roll out ⅔ of the pastry and line a 9-inch *deep* pie dish or springform pan. Then roll out the

remaining pastry onto waxed paper and make a circle
large enough to cover the dish. Chill pastry circle.

Sauté in medium skillet over medium-high heat, stirring
constantly:

  2 tablespoons butter
  1 small head cabbage, coarsely shredded
  1 yellow onion, peeled and chopped

Add, stirring frequently:

  ⅛ teaspoon marjoram
  ⅛ teaspoon tarragon
  ⅛ teaspoon basil
  salt, to taste
  ⅛ teaspoon freshly ground black pepper

Allow mixture to cook until cabbage is wilted and onions
are soft. Remove from skillet and set aside. Sauté in the
same pan for 5 or 6 minutes, stirring constantly:

  2 tablespoons butter
  ½ pound mushrooms, sliced

On the bottom of the pie shell, spread:

  4 ounces softened cream cheese

Top cheese with a layer of:

  4-5 hard-boiled eggs, sliced

Sprinkle eggs with:

  ⅛ teaspoon dried dill weed

Cover with cabbage, mushroom mixture, and the circle
of pastry. Press pastry together tightly at edges and flute
them. With a sharp knife, cut a few short slashes
through the top crust. Bake at 400° for 15 minutes, then
turn the temperature down to 350° and continue baking
for another 20-25 minutes or until the crust is light
brown.

Italian Vegetable Casserole

Serves: 8

Preparation time: 35 minutes
Baking time: 1½ hours

Preheat oven to 375°. Finely chop and mix together:

2 medium carrots
2 stalks celery
3 large cloves garlic

Add:

½ cup minced fresh parsley
2 teaspoons oregano
salt and black pepper, to taste

Oil a 4-quart casserole dish with olive oil and place in layers, alternating with the carrot and celery mixture:

3 medium red onions, thinly sliced
3 medium red or green bell peppers, cut into ¼-inch rings
4 medium red potatoes, cut into ⅛-inch rounds
4 medium zucchini, cut into ⅛-inch rounds

Drizzle each layer and the top of the casserole with:

olive oil (approximately ⅓ cup)

Bake at 375° for 1½ hours until tender. If the top gets too brown, cover dish with foil. Stir well before serving, and pour off any excess oil.

Stuffed Potatoes

Serves: 6

Preparation time: 40 minutes
Baking time: 20 minutes (not including time to bake potatoes)

Preheat oven to 350°. Bake until tender when pricked
with a fork:

6 large baking potatoes (3½ pounds)*

Cool potatoes and make a 2-3-inch cut lengthwise.
Scoop out the insides and place in a large bowl. Set the
skins aside.

Remove the tough stems, coarsely chop, and steam until
tender:

**1-1½ large bunches of kale (if kale is unavailable,
use a little over 1 pound of cabbage)**

Cook in a heavy saucepan until tender:

5 small leeks, chopped (white part only)
1¼-1½ cups whipping cream

Mash the potatoes, then add kale-leek mixture and:

3 tablespoons minced fresh parsley
1 cube butter, melted (½ cup)
salt and black pepper, to taste

Fill potato skins with mashed potato mixture and place
in a baking dish. Bake at 350° until potatoes are heated
throughout (about 20 minutes).

Variation:

Sprinkle tops with:

grated Gruyère cheese

Please note:

*If you use left-over baked potatoes, they mash more
easily if warmed.

Scalloped Potatoes
with Cheese and Broccoli

Serves: 5-8

Preparation time: 30-35 minutes
Baking time: 1½ hours

Preheat oven to 350°. Slice into ⅛-inch to ¼-inch slices:

4-5 baking potatoes (2½ pounds)

Steam until tender:

1½ cups chopped broccoli

In a buttered, *deep* 8-inch square pan, layer in the following order:

⅓ of the sliced potatoes
1½ tablespoons butter—dotted over the potatoes
⅛ teaspoon salt
⅛ teaspoon garlic powder
1½ tablespoons flour
½ cup grated medium cheddar cheese
1 tablespoon freshly grated Parmesan cheese
½ cup thinly sliced onions
freshly ground black pepper

Repeat the above, using steamed broccoli instead of onions. Top with remaining potatoes. Pour over mixture:

2½ cups milk

Sprinkle top with:

1 tablespoon freshly grated Parmesan cheese or more, to taste
paprika

Bake for 1½ hours at 350°.

Spicy Potato Casserole

Serves: 6-8

A good company dish.

Preparation time: 40-45 minutes
Baking time: 15-20 minutes

Preheat oven to 400°. Cook in salted water until tender, then drain:

8 medium-large potatoes (about 4½ pounds), cut into small cubes

While potatoes are cooking, grate:

2 cups (packed) cheddar cheese

Finely chop and set aside:

3 green onions, including tops
¼ cup fresh parsley
1 medium ripe tomato, peeled and seeded
1 stalk celery

When potatoes are done, drain and mash them with:

6 tablespoons butter
1⅜ teaspoons garlic powder
1 teaspoon salt or, to taste
¼ teaspoon cayenne
¼ teaspoon black pepper
1 cup cream

Add vegetables and 1 cup of the grated cheese to potatoes. Spoon mixture into buttered 9-inch by 12-inch casserole dish, or large oven-proof baking dish. Top with the remaining cup of cheese. Bake at 400° for 15-20 minutes or until cheese is golden brown.

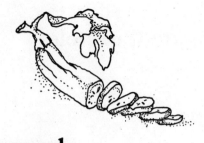

Zucchini Casserole

Serves: 8-10

An excellent company dish.

Preparation time: 45 minutes
Baking time: 30 minutes

Preheat oven to 350°. In an oiled 9-inch by 12-inch baking dish layer the following:

First layer—steam until crisp-tender:

7-8 cups zucchini (about 3 pounds), cut in ¼-inch rounds

Second layer—a mixture of:

**1 pint cottage cheese
1 pint sour cream
1 cup freshly grated Parmesan cheese
¼ teaspoon onion powder
¾ teaspoon garlic powder
4 rounded tablespoons minced fresh parsley
1½ teaspoons dried dill weed
¾ teaspoon salt
½ teaspoon black pepper
1 egg, beaten**

Third layer—sauté in medium skillet until transparent:

**3 tablespoons olive oil
2 medium-large onions, chopped**

Add and cook until nearly all the liquid is absorbed:

**1 pound mushrooms, sliced
2 tablespoons tamari**

Fourth layer—a mixture of:
   1 cup whole wheat bread crumbs
   4 tablespoons melted butter
   1¼ teaspoons basil
   1¼ teaspoons marjoram
   ¼ teaspoon garlic powder
   3 rounded tablespoons minced fresh parsley

Bake at 350° for 30 minutes.

Variations:

1. Add to bread crumb mixture:

   8 tablespoons freshly grated Parmesan cheese

2. For a thicker bread crumb topping, increase the amount of bread crumbs and adjust seasonings and butter.

Stuffed Zucchini   Serves: 4

Preparation time: 45 minutes
Baking time: 30-40 minutes

   Trim off ends and slice in half lengthwise:
      8 small zucchini (about 5 inches long) or 4 large zucchini

Scoop out insides of zucchini and chop, leaving a shell about ¼-inch thick. Set aside squash shells. In a large skillet, sauté with chopped zucchini over medium heat for a few minutes:

  1 tablespoon butter
  ¼ pound mushrooms, chopped
  1 tomato, chopped
  ½ large onion, finely chopped
  1 clove garlic, minced
  pinch thyme
  ⅛ teaspoon rosemary
  ¼ teaspoon basil

Increase heat to medium-high and cook, stirring frequently for 10 minutes until the liquid is reduced to ⅓ of the original amount. Preheat oven to 350°.

While sautéeing, mix in a large bowl:

  2 eggs, beaten
  ¾ cup cottage cheese
  3 tablespoons fresh whole wheat bread crumbs (less than 1 slice)
  1 tablespoon tamari
  dash Worcestershire sauce
  ½ cup grated sharp cheddar cheese
  ¼ cup chopped walnuts

Place zucchini halves in buttered 11-inch by 13-inch dish. Stuff zucchini generously. Sprinkle with:

  3 rounded tablespoons finely grated fresh Parmesan cheese

Bake at 350° for 30-40 minutes, depending on the size of the zucchini.

Squash and Spinach Casserole   Serves: 6

Colorful and festive.

Preparation time: 55 minutes
Baking time: 25 minutes

Preheat oven to 375°. Combine in medium skillet and sauté until toasted (about 5 minutes):

3 tablespoons melted butter
2 cups (packed) fresh whole wheat bread crumbs
1 teaspoon garlic powder

Combine in a bowl:

1 cup cottage cheese
½ teaspoon basil
½ teaspoon thyme
¼ teaspoon powdered rosemary
½ teaspoon oregano

Add bread crumb mixture. Using the same skillet, lightly sauté until almost tender:

4 tablespoons butter
6 medium crookneck squash (cut into ⅛-inch rounds)

Place sautéed squash in shallow casserole dish. Sprinkle with:

salt and black pepper, to taste

Top with ½ of bread crumb mixture. Using the same skillet, cover and steam 1 to 2 minutes or until wilted:

2 tablespoons butter
2 bunches well-washed spinach (leaves only)

Top bread crumbs with drained spinach. Sprinkle with:

salt and black pepper, to taste

Bake uncovered at 375° for 15 minutes. Cover spinach

with remaining bread crumb mixture. Then top with:

3 medium tomatoes (cut into ½-inch slices)
1 cup (packed) shredded cheddar cheese

Bake for an additional 10 minutes or until cheese is melted.

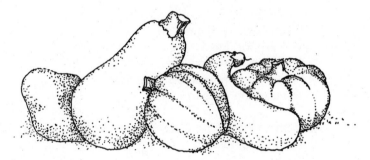

Stuffed Squash

Serves: 6

Preparation time: 20-30 minutes
Baking time: 20-25 minutes

Preheat oven to 350°. Cover with salted water, bring to a boil, then lower heat and cook covered until almost tender (20-30 minutes):

3 large chayote squash*, cut in half lengthwise

While squash cooks, sauté until golden:

½ cup butter
1 medium onion, minced

Drain and cool the squash. Discard fibers (flat, hard sections). Scoop pulp into a medium bowl. Set squash shells aside. Add onion to mashed squash pulp and mix well, adding the following seasonings, to taste:

celery salt
Spike (available at health food stores)
salt
black pepper

While squash is cooking, prepare the following:

1½ cups grated cheddar cheese
1 cup whole wheat bread crumbs

Add cheese and bread crumbs to squash mixture and fill shells. Sprinkle with:

½ cup whole wheat bread crumbs

Top with:

6 tablespoons freshly grated Parmesan cheese

Bake at 350° for 20-25 minutes until browned.

Please note:

*This squash is sometimes called vegetable pear. You can also use zucchini or crookneck squash. These take less time to cook.

Cabbage Casserole

Serves: 4-6

Preparation time: 50 minutes
Baking time: 50-60 minutes

Preheat oven to 350°. Spread in 2½-quart casserole dish:

9 cups (packed) coarsely shredded cabbage (about 1½ large heads—we prefer the leafy, Napa variety)

Season with:

salt and black pepper

Cover cabbage with:

3 medium tomatoes, peeled, seeded, and chopped

Cook according to the package instructions until crisp, then drain on a paper towel:

one 5-ounce package stripples (available in health food stores) or, to taste

Crumble stripples over tomatoes. Sauté until wilted:

1 tablespoon butter
1½ large onions, coarsely chopped

Remove onions and place on top of stripples. In medium skillet, melt:

2 tablespoons butter

Whisk in slowly:

3 tablespoons whole wheat pastry flour

When the flour has browned, gradually add, stirring constantly but do not boil:

⅔ cup milk

Remove from heat and add:

⅔ cup sour cream
salt and black pepper, to taste

Spoon sauce over cabbage mixture. Sprinkle top with:

¾ pound grated Muenster cheese

Cover casserole dish with foil and bake at 350° for
20 minutes. Remove foil and continue baking for
30-40 minutes, or until cabbage is tender.

Nutty Cornbread Loaf

Serves: 10-12

A good way to use up leftover cornbread!

Preparation time: 1 hour 15 minutes (much less with food processor)
Baking time: 2-2½ hours

Preheat oven to 350-375°. Blend in blender:

1½ cups hot water
5 Vegex vegetable bouillon cubes

When the cubes are dissolved, add, blend well, and set
aside:

4 medium tomatoes, chopped
6 eggs
¼ cup tamari
¼ teaspoon cayenne
3½ teaspoons sage
1 teaspoon thyme
1 teaspoon marjoram
1 teaspoon savory
1 teaspoon rosemary
1 teaspoon salt
1 teaspoon black pepper

Sauté in large skillet over medium heat until golden:

1½ cubes butter (¾ cup)
3 medium onions, chopped
3 large cloves garlic, minced
2 cups chopped celery
3 cups chopped mushrooms

Combine blender mixture and sautéed vegetables in large bowl. Add and mix well:

¾ cup finely grated carrots
1 cup minced fresh parsley
1¼ cups chopped toasted walnuts
½ cup ground walnuts
½ cup ground toasted sunflower seeds
6 cups dry cornbread crumbs*
4 cups toasted whole wheat bread crumbs

Spoon mixture into well-buttered 9-inch by 13-inch casserole dish. Bake at 350-375° for 2-2½ hours or until done. Serve with Cashew Gravy (page 158). Leftovers make tasty sandwiches.

Please note:

*If using our cornbread recipe (page 171), decrease amount of honey to 2½ tablespoons and omit poppy seeds.

Pakoras

Serves: 6-8

Deep fried vegetable croquettes with Indian spices.

Preparation time: 50 minutes
Frying time: 30 minutes

Grate or mince:

4 cups fresh spinach (leaves only)
2 cups cauliflower

Add:

1 tablespoon cumin powder
1 tablespoon turmeric
1 tablespoon coriander
¾ teaspoon cayenne
⅜ teaspoon ground cloves
⅜ teaspoon cardamon
¾ teaspoon cinnamon
⅜ teaspoon curry powder
4 large cloves garlic, pressed
1 tablespoon finely grated fresh ginger
1 tablespoon salt
¼ cup lemon juice
½ cup chopped Ortega green chiles

Add and mix well, forming a medium-thick batter:

3 cups garbanzo flour or more, as needed
water, if needed

Drop batter by spoonfuls into:

**1 quart hot peanut oil (use processed commercial
variety)**

Fry pakoras until dark golden brown. Remove with slotted spoon and drain on paper towels. Serve hot.

Samosa Filling

Serves: 6-8

In India this dish is traditionally used as a filling for samosas (see following recipe), but we also enjoy it as a main dish, similar to curry.

Preparation time: 45-50 minutes

Boil until tender:

9 medium potatoes, cut into large chunks

Allow potatoes to cool, then dice and set aside. While potatoes are cooking, sauté in large skillet over medium heat until onions are soft:

3 tablespoons butter
3 medium onions, finely chopped
1 tablespoon grated fresh ginger
1 tablespoon curry powder
1 tablespoon basil
1½ teaspoons coriander
1½ teaspoons turmeric
1½ teaspoons cinnamon
1 teaspoon ground cloves
¾ teaspoon cayenne

Add and sauté for a few minutes, stirring well:

6 small tomatoes, sliced
1 tablespoon salt
1½ teaspoons chile powder

Add and cook gently for 10 minutes:

3 cups fresh or frozen peas

Add the diced cooked potatoes and cook until almost dry. Then add and stir in:

3 tablespoons lemon or lime juice

Dough for Samosas

Makes: 12-15 samosas

A flaky, stuffed Indian pastry.

Preparation time: 10 minutes (does not include rolling out and stuffing)
To make ghee: 5-8 minutes

Mix together to form firm dough:

2 cups whole wheat pastry flour
1 teaspoon salt
2 tablespoons melted ghee*
5 tablespoons yogurt (add more yogurt if needed)

Knead dough until soft (but not sticky). You can knead this dough roughly. It should be pliable but not elastic. Roll out into 5-inch to 7-inch rounds. Cut rounds in half and form into triangles. Form each triangle into a cone, place stuffing in cone, fold over top, and seal edges with yogurt. Deep fry until dark golden brown in:

hot peanut oil (use processed commercial varieties)

Please note:

*To make ghee, melt over medium heat, skimming off milk solids as they bubble up:

2 cubes butter

Vegetable Curry

Serves: 6-8

Preparation time: 25-30 minutes

Sauté in large skillet over medium-high heat until seeds pop:

¼ cup peanut oil
4 teaspoons black mustard seeds

Lower heat. Add and continue to cook until onions are wilted:

2 large onions, chopped
4 teaspoons cumin seed
4 teaspoons turmeric
2 teaspoons coriander
2 teaspoons salt
½ teaspoon cayenne

Stir in:

10 cups cooked mixed vegetables (a good
   combination is cauliflower, broccoli and peas.
   You may also use leftover vegetables.)
1 cup yogurt

Simmer until vegetables are warmed throughout.

Cauliflower Curry

Serves: 4

Preparation time: 35 minutes

Sauté in large skillet until onions are soft:
¼-½ cup butter
1 large onion, diced

Add:
2 teaspoons black mustard seeds

When seeds begin to pop, add:
2 cloves garlic, minced
2 teaspoons fresh grated ginger
1 tablespoon cumin powder
1 tablespoon plus 1 teaspoon curry powder (for a
slightly milder flavor, use only 1 tablespoon curry
powder)
½ teaspoon salt

Add, cover, and simmer until cauliflower is done:
1 large cauliflower, chopped or separated into florets
½ cup water

Add and simmer until cauliflower is done:
2 large tomatoes, cut up, or 1 medium can
(approximately 15½ ounces) tomatoes (without
juice)

When nearly done, add:
1½ teaspoons lemon juice

Serve with rice.

Potato Curry with Peas

Serves: 3-4

A simple, light curry.

Preparation time: 25 minutes

Boil for 10 minutes or until tender when pierced with a fork, then drain:

4 cups diced potatoes (3-4 medium potatoes)

Cook, then drain:

1¼ cups petite peas

Set potatoes and peas aside. In a large skillet over medium-low heat, melt:

6 tablespoons butter (¾ stick)

Mix in and cook for 1 minute:

2 tablespoons curry powder

Then add:

½ cup half and half
salt, to taste

Add peas and potatoes to the curry sauce. Heat thoroughly. Garnish with:

1-2 tablespoons chopped fresh parsley

Potato-Mushroom Curry

Serves: 6-8

Preparation time: 35-40 minutes

Sauté over low heat in large covered saucepan until thoroughly cooked (20-25 minutes):

¼ cup peanut oil
3 large onions, chopped
1½ pounds mushrooms, chopped
one 7-ounce can chopped Ortega chiles
6 large cloves garlic, minced
4 teaspoons grated fresh ginger

While the above is cooking, steam until tender, then drain and set aside:

6 medium potatoes, cubed

After mushrooms are cooked, add:

1½ teaspoons turmeric
1½ teaspoons cumin powder
1½ teaspoons black pepper
2 teaspoons salt

Add potatoes to the curry mixture and heat through. Stir in and heat thoroughly:

½ cup sour cream

Spoonbread

Preparation time: 30 minutes
Baking time: 1 hour

Preheat oven to 375°. In a large heavy saucepan, mix together and bring to a boil, stirring occasionally:

**2 cups water
scant cup fine cornmeal
5 tablespoons butter
2 tablespoons honey
1 teaspoon salt**

Remove from heat and slowly whisk in until smooth:

**1¾ cups milk
4 eggs, beaten**

Whisk in:

1 tablespoon plus ¼ teaspoon baking powder

Cool the mixture. Fold in:

2 egg whites, beaten until stiff but not dry

Pour mixture into a greased 2½-quart baking dish. Bake at 375° until puffed and golden or until a knife inserted in center comes out clean. Serve immediately.

Variation:

Stir into the mixture together with milk and eggs:

1½ cups (packed) grated sharp cheddar cheese

Mushroom Polenta

Serves: 6

An excellent company dish, well worth the preparation time.

Preparation time: 1 hour
Cooking time: 2 hours
Baking time: 1½ hours
(Polenta and sauce can be made ahead of time and assembled and baked when needed.)

Mix well:

2½ cups cold water
1½ cups polenta meal (very coarse corn meal,
available at health food and specialty stores)

Add mixture by spoonfuls to:

2½ cups boiling water

Add and stir thoroughly:

1¾ teaspoons salt

Cook mixture in double boiler (uncovered) over medium-low heat without stirring for 1½ hours. Butter a *deep* 8-inch or 9-inch square oven-proof pan and spoon polenta into it. Smooth top of mixture and let cool until firm. When completely set, run a knife along edges and turn out onto a large cookie sheet. With a sharp knife or string, split polenta into 3 even layers. Set aside. Meanwhile, prepare sauce and cheese, as follows:

Sauté until golden and set aside:

1 cube butter (½ cup)
1½ large onions, chopped
3 large cloves garlic, minced

Wash and drain several times:

1½ ounces dried mushrooms

Soak mushrooms for 15 minutes in:

1½ cups hot water (drain and save the water)

Strain the water through several layers of cheese cloth 2-3 times and add, stirring until dissolved:

2 unsalted vegetable bouillon cubes

Set the broth aside. Chop the reconstituted dried mushrooms, discarding tough stems, and add them to:

2 cups (packed) coarsely chopped fresh mushrooms
2 rounded tablespoons finely minced fresh parsley
1½ teaspoons thyme
1½ teaspoons basil
scant ¼ teaspoon nutmeg

Add mixture to the sautéed onions and cook for 10 minutes or until mushrooms are tender. Add the mushroom broth and continue to cook over medium-high heat until liquid is reduced by ¾ (about 30 minutes).

Then add:
> ½ cup cream
> salt and black pepper, to taste

While the mixture is cooking, thinly slice:
> ¾ pound Jack cheese

Prepare:
> 2 cups grated fresh Parmesan cheese
> ½ cup toasted whole wheat bread crumbs

Preheat oven to 350°. Butter the baking dish again and spread the bread crumbs on the bottom. Lay 1 slice of polenta on top of bread crumbs. Cover with ⅓ of the sliced Jack cheese, then ⅓ of the mushroom sauce, and top with ⅓ of the grated Parmesan cheese. Repeat the layers until all the ingredients are used, ending with the grated Parmesan cheese. Bake covered at 350° for 1 hour, then uncover and continue baking for ½ hour longer. (Dish will be very full.)

Please note:
> If polenta layers fall apart in handling, gently piece them together. When you serve it, it *won't* fall apart.

Zucchini Patties

Serves: 4-6

A *light vegetable burger.*

Preparation time: 45 minutes

Steam until tender:
   2 cups (packed) coarsely grated zucchini

Sauté in medium skillet until soft:
   2 tablespoons oil
   3 green onions, chopped (including tops)

Add to sautéed onions:
   2 tablespoons (packed) minced fresh parsley
   1 teaspoon basil

Combine in separate bowl:
   1 cup (packed) fresh whole wheat bread crumbs
   ¼ cup (packed) toasted sunflower meal*
   ¼ cup cooked bulgur wheat or rice
   ½ teaspoon salt

Stir in:
   2 beaten egg yolks

Combine all of the above ingredients. Beat until stiff, then fold into zucchini mixture:
   whites of 2 eggs

Drop batter by spoonfuls onto lightly greased skillet and spread to form patties. Brown on both sides over medium heat. Serve with noodles or pilaf.

Please note:
   *Toast sunflower seeds in dry frying pan over medium heat, stirring constantly until browned, then grind in blender until the consistency of fine meal.

Spicy
Vegetable Croquettes   Makes: 20-25 croquettes

Preparation time: 50 minutes (much less with a food processor)
Frying time: 30-35 minutes

Grate or finely mince:

6 cups of the following raw vegetable combination: cauliflower, fresh spinach, onion, mushrooms, and potatoes (adjust quantity of each vegetable to suit your taste)

Add to vegetables:

2½ teaspoons cumin powder
2½ teaspoons turmeric
2½ teaspoons coriander
½ teaspoon cayenne or more, to taste (depending on how hot you like it)
3 large cloves garlic, pressed
3 teaspoons finely grated fresh ginger
3 teaspoons salt
½ cup lemon juice

Add and mix well with vegetables:

3 cups garbanzo (chick pea) flour (no substitute works nearly as well)

Mix well, forming a medium-thick batter, adding water or more flour as needed for croquette to hold its shape. Heat in Dutch oven or large heavy saucepan:

1 quart peanut oil (use processed oil to avoid oil foaming and overflowing pan)

Drop batter by spoonfuls into hot oil. Fry in batches until dark golden brown and remove with a slotted spoon onto a paper towel to drain.

Sunburgers

Makes: 7 patties

Preparation time: 30 minutes (less if you use a food processor)
Baking time: 35 minutes

Preheat oven to 375°. Mix together:
  1½ cups ground sunflower seeds
  ½ cup grated carrots
  ½ cup finely chopped celery
  6 tablespoons minced onions
  2 tablespoons minced fresh parsley
  2 eggs
  1 teaspoon basil
  2 tablespoons tamari
  2 tablespoons melted butter
  1 teaspoon garlic powder

Drop mixture by large spoonfuls, forming patties, onto an
oiled baking sheet. Bake at 375° for 20 minutes on one
side and 10-15 minutes on the other side. Both sides
should be a medium brown color. Serve on buns with
mayonnaise, catsup, or your favorite condiments.

Sunny Sesame-Tofu Burgers

Serves: 6

A make-ahead low calorie meal.

Preparation time: 20 minutes
Baking time: 40 minutes

Preheat oven to 375°. Mix together in a large bowl:

**6 cakes tofu (1½ pounds) rinsed, squeezed, and
  kneaded**
⅓ cup sunflower seeds
¼ cup brown sesame seeds
1 stalk celery, minced
¼ cup minced onion

Add and knead together:

2 tablespoons tamari
**2 tablespoons Dr. Bronner's Liquid Bouillon (or
  1 vegetable bouillon cube dissolved in 2 tablespoons hot water)**
1½ teaspoons Spike (available at health food stores)
1 teaspoon garlic powder
**2 tablespoons dried or 6 tablespoons minced fresh
  parsley**

Add and gently mix:

3 cups alfalfa sprouts

Pack mixture firmly and evenly into a buttered baking
dish, approximately 6-inch by 10-inch. Sprinkle with
additional sesame seeds and pat down. Bake at 375° for
40 minutes. Cut into 3-inch by 3-inch "burgers", cool,
and store in the refrigerator.

To serve, spread Tahini Dressing (page 64) evenly on top
and reheat the burger for 10-20 minutes at 350°. Serve as
you would a burger.

Tofu-Spinach Combo   Serves: 4

If you don't like tofu, try this one!

Preparation time: 25-30 minutes

Sauté in large skillet over medium heat for 5 minutes:
2 tablespoons butter
1 large onion, chopped

Add and sauté for 8-10 minutes or until slightly brown:
2 cups bite-size tofu pieces

Add:
2 tablespoons tamari
1 teaspoon Vegit (available at health food stores)
pinch of cayenne

Add and stir until wilted (about 5-8 minutes):
1 pound fresh spinach, washed and chopped (leaves only)

Sprinkle with juice of:
1 large lemon

Serve over steamed brown rice.

Tofu Stroganoff

Serves: 4

Preparation time: 35 minutes

Rinse, then drain on paper towels to remove excess water:

1½ blocks tofu (18 ounces)

In a large skillet, sauté until onions are soft and transparent:

2 tablespoons butter
1 medium onion, chopped
10 mushrooms, thickly sliced
2 tablespoons dried chives
½-1 teaspoon garlic powder
¼ teaspoon salt
¼ teaspoon black pepper

Remove mixture from skillet and set aside. Add to skillet:

1 tablespoon butter plus 1 tablespoon vegetable oil

Brown tofu, sliced in strips, in 2 batches, using more butter and oil as needed. Add mushroom mixture to tofu. Just before serving, add:

1 cup sour cream
2-4 tablespoons tamari
1-2 tablespoons cooking sherry

Cook over low heat. Do not boil. To thin sauce, add more sour cream. Adjust sherry, to taste. Serve over noodles.

Scrambled Tofu

Serves: 2-3

Very much like scrambled eggs.

Preparation time: 15 minutes

Mash with a fork:
2 packages tofu (18 ounces)

Melt in medium skillet over medium-low heat:
3 tablespoons butter

Sauté tofu in butter, then add:
1½-2 tablespoons tamari
¼ teaspoon turmeric
1 teaspoon onion powder

Variations:
Add one or more of the following:
curry powder
herbs
sautéed chopped vegetables

Smothered Tofu

Serves: 4-5

Delicious on rice or mashed potatoes.

Preparation time: 50 minutes

Sauté in large skillet over medium heat for 5 minutes, stirring occasionally:
½ cube butter (4 tablespoons)
1½ cups chopped onions

Add and continue to sauté until tender, stirring occasionally:

½ pound mushrooms, sliced

Remove mixture from pan and set aside. Mix together in a bag for shaking:

½ cup nutritional yeast (flaked variety)
½ cup whole wheat pastry flour

Mix in a bowl:

¼ cup tamari plus enough water to make ⅓ cup
1 teaspoon garlic powder
½ teaspoon basil
¼ teaspoon marjoram
¼ teaspoon thyme
pinch of cayenne

Cut into bite-size pieces:

2-2¼ pounds firm tofu

Melt in large skillet over medium heat:

½ cube butter

While melting butter, dip tofu quickly into tamari mixture, then place it in the bag with flour-yeast mixture and shake. Brown tofu in melted butter, stirring occasionally. (Tofu tends to crumble while cooking.) Mix together:

2 cups boiling water
1 unsalted vegetable bouillon cube

Add broth to browned tofu. Stir in onions and mushrooms. Let simmer for 5-10 minutes.

Baked Tofu with Cheese

Serves: 4-6

Preparation time: 15 minutes
Baking time: 20-25 minutes

Preheat oven to 350°. Slice into pieces ½-inch thick and arrange in a single layer in an oiled 9-inch by 12-inch baking dish:

1½ pounds tofu

Poke holes in tofu with fork and sprinkle with:

6 tablespoons tamari sauce
½ teaspoon garlic powder

Cover with:

6 ounces cheddar cheese, grated

Bake at 350° until a crust forms on the melted cheese—about 20-25 minutes, depending on how crunchy you like it.

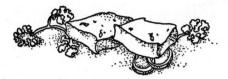

Tofu "Steaks"

Serves: 6

Preparation time: 23 minutes
Frying time: 35 minutes

To make marinade, mix together:
  ⅓ cup tamari
  ¼ cup cooking sherry
  2½ tablespoons grated fresh ginger
  2½ teaspoons garlic powder
  ½ cup water

Slice in pieces ¼-inch thick and marinate for
15 minutes, turning once:
  1½-2 pounds tofu

Brown tofu in 2 batches in large skillet over medium
heat, using:
  butter and oil

Keep first batch in a warm oven while second batch
cooks.

Nutty Cheese Cutlets
with Gravy

Serves: 6-8

Preparation time: 50 minutes
Baking time: 30-35 minutes

Preheat oven to 375°. Soften and mash:

one 8-ounce package cream cheese

Stir in:

1½ cups chopped onions
¼ pound grated cheddar cheese (about ¾ cup)
3 eggs, beaten
1 cup chopped walnuts
1 cup cracker crumbs (about 4 large crackers. Ak-Mak, available at health food stores, work well)
1 teaspoon oregano

Press mixture into small patties and brown over medium-high heat for 1-2 minutes on each side in:

vegetable oil

Place patties single layer in baking dish. Mix together:

2 cans undiluted cream of mushroom soup (we use Campbell's)
1½ cups water
½ teaspoon garlic powder
¼ teaspoon oregano
¼ teaspoon beau monde
¼ teaspoon marjoram
¼ teaspoon thyme
¼ teaspoon sage

Pour ¾ of the sauce over the patties, covering each one, and bake at 375° for 20 minutes. Add the remainder of the sauce and bake for another 10-15 minutes. Delicious served with mashed potatoes or noodles.

Walnut Cheddar Loaf

Serves: 6-8

Delicious cold for sandwiches.

Preparation time: 40 minutes
Baking time: 1 hour

Preheat oven to 350°. Combine the following ingredients in a large bowl and set aside:

3 cups (packed) fresh whole wheat bread crumbs
1 cup (packed) ground walnuts
1 cup finely chopped walnuts
½ cup nutritional yeast
2 tablespoons tamari
½ cup tomato juice

Sauté in large skillet over medium heat until translucent:

4 tablespoons butter
3 large onions, finely chopped
3-4 large cloves garlic, minced

Combine all of the above with:

2 well-beaten eggs
1 cup (packed) grated cheddar cheese
1 teaspoon salt
½ teaspoon black pepper
2 tablespoons dried parsley or ¾ cup minced fresh
   parsley

Press into well-oiled loaf pan and bake at 350° for approximately 1 hour. Cover top of loaf with:

½ cup grated cheddar cheese

Bake for an additional 10 minutes or until cheese is bubbly. Serve as is, or with a gravy.

Spinach-Rice Casserole

Serves: 4-5

Excellent for light dinners or brunch.

Preparation time: 40-45 minutes
Baking time: 35 minutes

Cook for 40 minutes (see rice cooking instructions, page 82):
- ¾ cup brown rice
- 2 cups vegetable broth (1 salted vegetable bouillon cube dissolved in 2 cups boiling water)

After rice has cooked for half an hour, pre-heat oven to 350°. While rice is cooking, prepare:
- ½ cup grated cheddar cheese
- 2 tablespoons minced fresh parsley
- 1 pound fresh spinach, washed and chopped (leaves only)

Mix cooked rice with the above ingredients, adding:
- ¼ teaspoon garlic powder or more, to taste
- ¼ teaspoon black pepper
- 2 eggs, beaten

Spoon mixture into oiled casserole dish or 8-inch square pan. Combine and top with:
- 4 rounded tablespoons finely grated fresh Parmesan cheese
- 2 tablespoons butter, melted
- ½ cup fresh whole wheat bread crumbs

Bake at 350° for 35 minutes.

Quick Millet Pilaf

Serves: 4-6

Preparation time: 35 minutes

Bring to a boil:
4½-5 cups water (depending on how moist you like it)

Stir in, cover, and simmer over low heat:
2 cups millet
2 unsalted Huegli vegetable bouillon cubes

Meanwhile, lightly sauté in large skillet over medium heat for 5 minutes, stirring occasionally:
2 tablespoons vegetable oil
3 medium-large carrots, sliced

Then add and sauté for 3 more minutes:
handful of cashews, coarsely chopped
1 large onion, chopped

Add and continue to sauté until onions are soft and transparent:
2-3 cloves garlic, minced

When millet is almost dry (about 30 minutes), stir in sautéed mixture and:
½ cup grated cheese (Jack or cheddar)
½ cup nutritional yeast (flaked variety)
2 teaspoons basil
tamari, to taste
dash of cayenne

Stir well and serve. This dish should be moist, not dry and fluffy.

Enchilada Casserole

Serves: 6-9

Preparation time: 45 minutes (including sauce)
Baking time: 30 minutes

Preheat oven to 350°. In a 9-inch by 12-inch casserole dish, assemble in layers, in two stacks, side by side, using half of the following ingredients for each stack:

8 warmed tortillas
2 ripe avocados, mashed and mixed with
6 tablespoons sour cream
two 4-ounce cans chopped Ortega green chiles
5 cups grated cheddar or Jack cheese (save a little to
   sprinkle over top)
½ cup sliced black olives

Pour enchilada sauce (see below) over each layer and over top. Sprinkle the top of each tortilla stack with a little cheese. Bake at 350° for 30 minutes. Serve with:

sour cream and chopped green onions

Enchilada Casserole Sauce

Makes: 4-5 cups

Sauté in large saucepan over medium heat until golden:
4 tablespoons olive oil
2 large cloves garlic, minced
2 medium onions, finely chopped

Add and cook until boiling:
two 10-ounce cans Las Palmas red chile sauce
two 7-ounce cans Ortega green chile salsa

Chile Rellenos

Preparation time: 1 hour

Cut into long strips:
1 pound Jack cheese

Stuff cut cheese into each chile in:
three 7-ounce cans whole Ortega green chiles

Set chiles aside. Beat until stiff:
13 egg whites

Beat until thick:
8 egg yolks

Gently fold egg yolks into whites. Fold in:
2½ tablespoons whole wheat pastry flour

Heat in large skillet:
½ inch oil

Spoon enough egg batter into oil to hold a chile. Place a chile in center of batter and cover it completely, using more batter. Fry until golden brown on each side.

Arrange chiles on serving platter and serve with salsa, or place in 9-inch by 13-inch pan and top with:
one 11-ounce can enchilada sauce or 1-2 cups of Enchilada Casserole Sauce (opposite page)

Sprinkle with grated cheese if desired and bake at 350° until heated through.

Chile-Egg Puff Casserole

Serves: 6-8

Preparation time: 20 minutes
Baking time: 25-35 minutes

Preheat oven to 375°. Butter a 9-inch by 12-inch dish and arrange in a single layer:

10 whole Ortega green chiles (a little more than one 4-ounce can)

Thinly slice and spread on top of chiles:

¾ pound cheese (½ Jack and ½ cheddar)

Mix until well-blended and pour over chiles and cheese:

6 eggs
1¾ cups milk
¼ teaspoon salt
⅛ teaspoon black pepper
¼ teaspoon garlic powder

Bake at 375° for 25-35 minutes. Top with:

green taco sauce and/or sour cream
sliced black olives

Egg Puff

Serves: 6-8

A mild egg, chile, and cheese dish.

Preparation time: 10-15 minutes
Baking time: 35 minutes

Preheat oven to 350°. Beat:
10 large eggs

Add and mix well:
½ cup whole wheat pastry flour
½ teaspoon baking powder

Mix in:
1 pint small curd cottage cheese
1 pound Jack or mild cheddar cheese, grated
¼ teaspoon salt
one 7-ounce can chopped Ortega green chiles

Spoon into 9-inch by 13-inch pan and bake at 350° for 35 minutes or until eggs are set. Serve with salsa.

Easy Cheese Soufflé

Serves: 4-5

Preparation time: 30-35 minutes
Baking time: 25-30 minutes

Preheat oven to 375°. Melt in medium saucepan over low heat:

6 tablespoons butter

Stir in:

6 tablespoons whole wheat pastry flour
¾ teaspoon salt
½ teaspoon black pepper
⅛ teaspoon cayenne

Slowly add and cook, whisking constantly until thick and smooth:

2 cups milk

Add and mix thoroughly:

1 cup (packed) grated sharp cheddar cheese

Remove mixture from heat and add gradually, whisking the entire time:

6 egg yolks, beaten

Gently fold in:

6 egg whites, stiffly beaten

Spoon into a buttered straight-sided or soufflé dish and bake at 375° for 25-30 minutes. Serve immediately or soufflé will fall. (Avoid drafts!) Excellent with Yogurt-Cheese Sauce (page 151) or Tomato-Sour Cream Sauce (page 146).

Variation:

Before adding soufflé mixture, layer in baking dish:

steamed or sautéed asparagus or broccoli

Mushroom Baked Eggs

Serves: 4-5

Preparation time: 25-30 minutes

Preheat oven to broil. Sauté in large skillet over medium heat until onions are golden and most of the liquid has evaporated:

6 tablespoons butter
2 medium onions, chopped
2 large cloves garlic, minced
½ pound mushrooms, sliced

Spoon mushroom mixture into 8-inch square pan. Make 8 slight indentations and drop in:

8 eggs

Sprinkle each egg with the following, seasoning to taste:

oregano
salt and black pepper
cayenne
basil

Place eggs under broiler for several minutes and watch closely. When they are almost done, remove from broiler and cover with:

1 cup (packed) grated cheddar cheese

Return to broiler until cheese is melted. (Be careful not to let cheese burn.)

Savory Broccoli Quiche

Serves: 4-6

Yeast adds a rich full-bodied flavor.

Preparation time: 50 minutes (including making crust)
Baking time: 45 minutes

Preheat oven to 400°. Prepare a basic single pastry crust
(page 190). Line a deep pie pan or a deep quiche pan
with pastry and prick with a fork. Bake at 400° for 8-10
minutes. To make filling, steam until tender, then drain:

1 medium bunch of broccoli, chopped (about 2 cups)

Meanwhile, sauté in medium skillet over medium heat
until golden:

4 tablespoons butter
1 medium-large onion, chopped

Add and blend well:

3 tablespoons nutritional yeast

Cook mixture over low heat for several minutes, remove
from heat, and cool slightly. While onion mixture is
cooling, prepare:

1½ cups (packed) grated Gruyère cheese

Place onion-yeast mixture on bottom of pre-baked pie
shell. Sprinkle with ¾ of the grated cheese. Top with
steamed broccoli. Combine:

4 eggs, beaten
1½ cups milk
¼ teaspoon salt
scant ½ teaspoon black pepper
⅛ rounded teaspoon nutmeg
scant ¼ teaspoon cayenne

Pour egg mixture over broccoli. Bake at 450° for 15
minutes, then turn heat down to 350° and add the rest of
the grated cheese. Continue baking for 30 more minutes
or until a knife inserted in center comes out clean.

Mushroom-Spinach Quiche

Serves: 6

Preparation time: 40 minutes
Baking time: 50 minutes
(See Savory Broccoli Quiche, page 136, for pie crust)

Preheat oven to 375°. To make filling, sauté in large skillet over medium heat for 5 minutes or until mushrooms are soft:

4 tablespoons butter
5 green onions, chopped (including tops)
¾ pound mushrooms, sliced
1½ teaspoons garlic powder

Add to mushroom mixture and cook until liquid is almost evaporated:

10 ounces fresh spinach or one 10-ounce package
frozen spinach, thawed and drained

Meanwhile, mix together:

4 eggs, beaten
1½ cups grated Swiss cheese
1¾ cups heavy cream or 1¾ cups half and half
¼ teaspoon nutmeg or, to taste
¼ teaspoon cayenne or, to taste
½ teaspoon salt or, to taste
½ teaspoon black pepper or, to taste

Combine all ingredients and pour into pre-baked pie shell. Sprinkle over top:

1½-3 tablespoons freshly grated Parmesan cheese
paprika

Bake at 375° for 40-50 minutes or until knife inserted in center comes out clean.

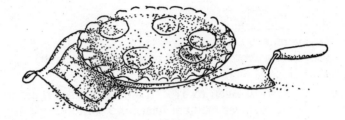

Spinach-Tomato Quiche

Serves: 4-6

Preparation time: 30-40 minutes
Baking time: 1½ hours
(See Savory Broccoli Quiche, page 136, for pie crust)

Preheat oven to 350°. Shred and set aside:
   1½ cups (packed) Swiss cheese

Sauté in large skillet over medium heat, for 3-5 minutes
or until spinach is wilted:
   2 tablespoons butter
   1 pound spinach (leaves only)
   ½ cup chopped green onions (including tops)
   1 clove garlic, minced

Mix together:
   4 large eggs, beaten
   1 cup milk
   1 teaspoon salt
   1 teaspoon basil
   ½ teaspoon celery seed
   ½ teaspoon dry mustard
   ½ teaspoon curry powder
   ½ teaspoon onion powder
   ⅛ teaspoon black pepper
   1 teaspoon arrowroot
   pinch of cayenne
   pinch of nutmeg

Slice and set aside:
   2 medium tomatoes

Layer in a pre-baked pie crust in the following order:
   **half of the shredded cheese
   spinach mixture
   remaining shredded cheese
   milk mixture
   sliced tomatoes**

Sprinkle on top of tomatoes:
   ¼-½ teaspoon dried basil

Bake at 350° for 1½ hours.

Hungarian Noodles

Serves: 4-6

Preparation time: 15-20 minutes
Baking time: 30 minutes

Preheat oven to 350°. Cook in salted water until almost tender:

½ pound fettucine noodles (sesame or soy-corn)

Drain and combine with:

1 cup cottage cheese
1 cup sour cream
¼ cup (packed) finely chopped green onions
2 large cloves garlic, minced
1 tablespoon poppy seeds
1 tablespoon tamari

Bake in an 8-inch square baking dish at 350° for 30 minutes. Sprinkle top with:

½ cup (packed) freshly grated Parmesan cheese
¼ teaspoon paprika

Bake for 5 minutes more or until cheese melts.

Mushroom Spaghetti

Serves: 5-6

Preparation time: 25 minutes

Cook until almost tender in salted water:

1 pound sesame spaghetti

While preparing spaghetti, sauté in medium skillet over medium heat and set aside:

3 tablespoons olive oil
1 pound mushrooms, sliced
¾ teaspoon salt
1 teaspoon black pepper

In a serving bowl, mix hot spaghetti with:

1 egg, beaten
7 tablespoons freshly grated Parmesan cheese
2 tablespoons butter
1 tablespoon olive oil

Top with sautéed mushrooms.

Variation:

Add one or both of the following:

onion sautéed in olive oil
cheese and an extra egg

Lasagna

Serves: 6-8

Preparation time: 1½ hours
Cooking time (sauce): 1 hour
Baking time: 45 minutes-1 hour

To make filling, sauté in large skillet over medium heat
for 5 minutes:

⅓ cup olive oil
1½ cups chopped onions
4 cloves garlic, minced

Add and sauté 5 minutes more:

1½ cups sliced zucchini, cut into ¼-inch rounds

Add and cook another 5 minutes or until mushrooms and
zucchini are tender:

6 cups sliced mushrooms (about 1 pound)
½ teaspoon basil
¼ teaspoon salt
⅛-¼ teaspoon black pepper
⅛ teaspoon cayenne

To cook noodles, cook in a large saucepan for 15 minutes
or until almost tender:

1 pound lasagna noodles (we prefer sesame)
1 tablespoon vegetable oil

Rinse under cold water and set aside.

Prepare cheeses:

4 ounces thinly sliced Jack cheese
10 ounces thinly sliced mozzarella cheese
¼-½ cup (packed) grated fresh Parmesan cheese
1⅓ cups ricotta cheese (a little less than 1 pound)

Preheat oven to 350°. To assemble, oil a *deep* 9-inch by
11-inch pan. Layer in pan in the following order:

1 cup tomato sauce (see below)
⅓ of the noodles
⅔ cup ricotta cheese
½ of the mushroom mixture
the Jack cheese
1 cup tomato sauce
1 tablespoon Parmesan cheese or more, to taste
half the remaining noodles
⅔ cup ricotta cheese
rest of mushroom mixture
4 ounces mozzarella cheese (less than half)
last of the noodles
1¾ cups tomato sauce
rest of mozzarella cheese

Top with:

remaining Parmesan cheese
⅓ cup sliced black olives

Bake at 350° for 45 minutes-1 hour.

To make tomato sauce (5 cups), sauté in large saucepan over medium heat for 5 minutes:

½ cup olive oil
2 cups finely chopped onions
3 cloves garlic, minced

Add and simmer for 1 hour:

2 large (28-ounce) cans tomatoes
6 ounces tomato paste
2 tablespoons minced fresh parsley
1 teaspoon salt
1½ tablespoons honey
1 rounded teaspoon oregano
1 rounded teaspoon basil
¼ teaspoon black pepper
1 cup water
⅛ teaspoon cayenne or, to taste

It's in your heart
  The songs of joy resound:
You'll hear but echoes
  In the world around.
Wind on a hill
    Sounds lonely if you're sad,
Free if you're free,
    Cheerful if you're glad.

Sauces,
Dips & Spreads

Tomato-Sour Cream Sauce   Makes: 7 cups

An unusual, versatile sauce.

Preparation time: 20-25 minutes
Cooking time: 30-35 minutes

Blanch (to remove skins) by dropping into boiling water:
   6 large tomatoes

After several minutes remove with slotted spoon and immediately plunge into cold water. Slip the skins (they come right off). Slice tomatoes and place in heavy saucepan. Add:
   4 tablespoons butter
   3 large onions, sliced into thin rounds, then cut in half

Cook over low heat for 30-35 minutes, stirring occasionally. When sauce is almost done, add the following seasonings to taste:
   salt
   black pepper
   garlic powder
   basil

After sauce has cooked, remove from heat and stir in:
   1 pint sour cream

Use as an omelet filling or as a sauce for fritata or pasta.

Summer Garden Spaghetti Sauce

Makes: 4-6 cups

Delicate fresh garden taste.

Preparation time: 40-45 minutes (much less if you use a food processor)
Cooking time: 4 hours

Sauté in large saucepan over medium heat for about 10 minutes:
- ½ cup olive oil
- 1½ large onions, chopped
- 5 large carrots, coarsely shredded
- 3 large cloves garlic, minced
- 5 stalks celery, finely chopped

Purée in blender:
- 8 large fresh tomatoes

Mix sautéed vegetables and tomatoes with:
- one 15-ounce can tomato sauce

Add:
- 1 bay leaf
- 1 teaspoon basil or more, to taste
- ½ teaspoon marjoram
- ¾ teaspoon salt
- ¼ teaspoon black pepper
- ½ teaspoon garlic powder
- 1 bunch fresh parsley, finely chopped

Simmer sauce uncovered for 2 hours, stirring occasionally. Remove the bay leaf and simmer for 2 more hours.

Spaghetti Sauce
with Mushrooms

Makes: 10-12 cups

A wonderful all-purpose sauce.

Preparation time: 50 minutes
Cooking time: 45 minutes-1 hour

Sauté in large saucepan over medium heat until onions
are transparent:

½ cup olive oil
4 medium onions, chopped
7 large cloves garlic, minced
4 large green bell peppers, chopped
¾ pound mushrooms, thickly sliced

Add and simmer for about an hour:

6 small bay leaves (remove after 30-35 minutes of
      cooking)
1 teaspoon garlic powder
4 pounds canned tomatoes with juice, coarsely chop-
      ped (if using fresh tomatoes, add a little tomato
      juice)
12 ounces tomato paste
2 tablespoons honey or, to taste
1½ teaspoons salt
1 teaspoon ground dried rosemary
1 teaspoon ground dried thyme
1 teaspoon ground dried oregano
1 tablespoon basil
1 teaspoon black pepper
1 teaspoon chile powder
½ teaspoon cumin powder
½ cup minced fresh parsley

Variations:

1. Add sautéed or steamed vegetables to sauce (eggplant, peas, zucchini, cauliflower). Add vegetables during last 20 minutes of cooking.

2. Add to pasta and mix well just before serving:
   ricotta cheese, to taste

Blender Pesto

Makes: ¾ cup

Preparation time: 15-20 minutes

Combine in blender at high speed:
2 cups fresh basil leaves (tear all but the smallest leaves in half and press into cup)
½ cup olive oil
2 tablespoons pine nuts (or walnuts)
2 cloves garlic, lightly crushed with the flat of a knife
½ teaspoon salt

Pour mixture into a bowl and stir in well:
½ cup plus 2 tablespoons freshly grated Parmesan cheese

Add:
3 tablespoons butter, softened at room temperature

Add pesto (to taste) to noodles, rice or soup. It's also delicious in omelets. Refrigerate left-over pesto by covering it with a thin layer of olive oil. To freeze, omit oil.

Tofu-Yogurt Sauce

Makes: 2¾ cups

An excellent, low-calorie sauce. Use as a vegetable dip or as a filling for enchiladas, manicotti, or lasagna.

Preparation time: 10 minutes

Blend until smooth (for tofu, a food processor works better than a blender):

1 pound tofu
2 tablespoons tahini
2 tablespoons red miso
4 teaspoons tamari
1 cup yogurt
2 tablespoons lemon juice
2 teaspoons onion powder
2 teaspoons garlic powder

Variation:

For a spicy sauce, add:

curry powder, to taste

Yogurt-Cheese Sauce

Makes: 3-4 cups

A versatile sauce that doubles as a spread.

Preparation time: 20-25 minutes

Melt over low heat:
   3 tablespoons butter

Add slowly, stirring constantly to keep mixture smooth:
   2-3 tablespoons whole wheat pastry flour (depending on how thick a sauce you want)

Cook mixture for a few minutes over low flame, stirring occasionally. Meanwhile, heat over low flame until hot but not boiling:
   1½ cups yogurt
   ½ teaspoon black pepper
   pinch of cayenne

Add yogurt mixture to butter and flour a little at a time, whisking constantly. Cook until sauce is thoroughly heated. Add, a little at a time, whisking constantly:
   2 cups (packed) grated, sharp cheddar cheese

After cheese melts, remove from heat and add:
   3 thinly sliced green onions (including tops)
   a few sautéed mushrooms (optional)

The mixture should be hot enough to cook the onions. Add onions sooner if more cooking is desired. Excellent over soufflés and steamed vegetables. Use cold as a spread for crackers.

Butter Sauce

Makes: ½ cup

A simple and delicious way to embellish vegetables.

Preparation time: 5 minutes

Melt:
   ¼ pound butter

Season with any of the following:
   1 teaspoon turmeric
   juice of 1 lemon with or without 1 tablespoon tamari
   pressed garlic clove lightly sautéed in butter
   1 teaspoon any dried herb or combination of herbs
   2 teaspoons light miso

Tamari-Garlic Sauce

Makes: 4 cups

Preparation time: 8-10 minutes

Combine in large saucepan and whisk together until smooth:
   ⅓-½ cup tamari (depending on how strong a tamari flavor you want)
   ½ teaspoon black pepper
   1 teaspoon garlic powder
   1½ cups buttermilk
   1½ cups sour cream
   ½ cup nutritional yeast

Cook over medium heat for 3-5 minutes or until heated through. Serve with noodles, millet or rice.

Sour Cream-
Mayonnaise Dip

Makes: a little over 2 cups

Preparation time: 15-20 minutes
Chilling time: overnight

Combine and mix well:

    1 cup sour cream
    1 cup mayonnaise
    ½ teaspoon salt
    ½ teaspoon paprika
    3 tablespoons grated onion
    ¼ teaspoon curry powder
    ½ tablespoon lemon juice
    ¼ cup (packed) fresh minced parsley
    1 large clove garlic, finely minced or pressed
    ½ teaspoon Worcestershire sauce

Chill overnight.

Variation:

Substitute for sour cream and mayonnaise:

    2 cups yogurt

Spicy Avocado
Sandwich Spread

Makes: 2¾ cups

Preparation time: 15-20 minutes

Mash in medium bowl:
   5 large avocados

Add:
   2 tablespoons plus ½ teaspoon lemon juice
   1 tablespoon tamari or more, to taste
   6 small cloves garlic, pressed
   6 tablespoons plain yogurt
   **4 tablespoons finely chopped green onions (including
      tops)**
   ¾ teaspoon cumin powder or more, to taste
   ¾ teaspoon chile powder or more, to taste
   salt, to taste

Serve on bread with sprouts, thinly sliced cheese, and
raw mushrooms.

Artichoke-Olive
Sandwich Spread

Makes: 3 cups

Preparation time: 15-20 minutes

Cream with mixer:
   2 cups soft cream cheese (about 1 pound)

Add and stir in:
> two 6-ounce jars marinated artichoke hearts, drained
>   and chopped (save oil)
> ½ cup (packed) chopped black olives
> 1 teaspoon onion powder
> 1 rounded teaspoon oregano or more, to taste
> 6 tablespoons artichoke oil

Serve as a dip or sandwich spread.

Variation:
> Instead of cream cheese use:
> > grated cheddar or Jack cheese

Eggplant Dip

Makes: 1½ cups

Preparation time: 20-30 minutes

Cut into ½-inch cubes and steam until soft:
> 1 medium eggplant

Mash the steamed eggplant and add:
> ½ cup yogurt
> 6 tablespoons sour cream
> 1 teaspoon salt
> ¼ teaspoon black pepper

Variation:
> For a spicier dip add:
> > 2 tablespoons tahini
> > 4 cloves garlic, pressed
> > ½ teaspoon coriander

Spicy Mid-Eastern Dip

Makes: 1 cup

Preparation time: 40 minutes

Peel and cut into ½-inch slices:
   1 large eggplant

In a large skillet, sauté eggplant over medium heat until browned and very soft in:
   4-6 tablespoons hot vegetable oil*

Drain on paper towels and set aside for 10 minutes. In large bowl, combine:
   3 tablespoons peanut butter
   3 tablespoons fresh lemon juice
   2 cloves garlic, minced or pressed

Add cooled eggplant to mixture and blend with spoon or blender. Season with:
   ⅛ teaspoon salt

Drain off excess oil, if any. Excellent as a dip for pita bread, crackers or crisp vegetables.

Please note:

   *The oil should be hot enough that the eggplant sizzles when placed in pan. Add more oil as needed.

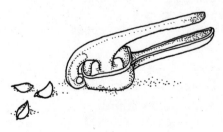

Guacamole

Makes: 1 cup

Preparation time: 10-15 minutes

In a medium bowl, mash:
1 large or 2 small avocados

Stir in:
1½ teaspoons freshly squeezed lemon juice
1 tablespoon finely minced green or white onion
⅛-¼ teaspoon salt
¼ teaspoon chile powder
¼ teaspoon cumin powder
1 green Ortega chile, chopped
1 clove garlic, minced or pressed
1 tablespoon sour cream
½ teaspoon chile salsa
pinch of coriander
1 small tomato, chopped (optional)

If you cover guacamole with plastic wrap, it will keep for 24 hours without discoloring. (Lay plastic directly onto guacamole.)

Yeast Gravy

Makes: 1 cup

Preparation time: 15-20 minutes

Melt in medium saucepan over medium heat:
3 tablespoons butter

Add and cook for 3 minutes:
3 tablespoons whole wheat pastry flour
2 tablespoons nutritional yeast (flaked variety)
¼ teaspoon thyme
¼ teaspoon savory
½ teaspoon tamari
pinch of black pepper
salt, to taste

Remove from heat and slowly whisk in, until smooth:
1½ cups vegetable stock (dissolve 1 unsalted vegetable bouillon cube in 1½ cups boiling water)

Return saucepan to heat and cook until thick.

Variation:
Remove from heat and add vegetable stock following above instructions. Then add:
½ cup sautéed onions
¼ rounded teaspoon garlic powder
pinch of marjoram

Cashew Gravy

Makes: 4 cups

Very rich.

Preparation time: 20-25 minutes

Sauté in large skillet over medium heat until golden:
6 tablespoons butter
1 medium onion, chopped

Stir in, cook for 3 minutes, stirring constantly:
6 tablespoons whole wheat pastry flour
1¼ cups finely ground raw cashews

Add slowly, whisking constantly until mixture is smooth:
3 unsalted vegetable bouillon cubes (dissolved in
4 cups boiling water)

Add:
5 tablespoons tamari
⅜ teaspoon garlic powder or more, to taste
black pepper, to taste

Bring gravy to a boil, then turn down heat and simmer until thick. Purée in blender in batches to ensure smoothness.

Variation:

Just before serving, add:
¼ cup chopped fresh parsley

Adjust the seasonings if necessary.

Without silence, what is song?
Without night, where is dawn?
Were it not for men's woes,
Who would smile at a rose?

Morning laughter, evening tears,
Snow and blossoms—all fade!
Joy must sing in the night
To face change unafraid.

Quick Breads

Lemon Scones

Makes: 20-24 scones

Preparation time: 40 minutes
Baking time: 12-15 minutes

Preheat oven to 450°. Sift together in medium bowl:

4 cups whole wheat pastry flour
4 teaspoons baking powder
1½ teaspoons baking soda
1 teaspoon salt

Stir in:

3½ tablespoons lemon rind

Cut in with a knife or pastry cutter until mixture resembles coarse meal:

⅓ cup cold vegetable shortening
⅓ cup cold butter

Mix together:

1½ cups buttermilk
4 tablespoons honey

Make a well in the center of flour mixture and pour in sweetened buttermilk. Toss with fork until blended. Knead dough on floured board until smooth (3-5 times). Use flour as needed to keep dough from sticking to board. Roll dough out (adding flour as needed) to ½-inch thick. Cut into 2-inch to 2½-inch rounds. Arrange rounds on ungreased cookie sheet 1 inch apart. Brush tops with:

half and half

Bake at 450° for 12-15 minutes until golden. Serve immediately with butter and jam.

Whole Wheat Biscuits

Makes: 24 biscuits

Tender and flaky.

Preparation time: 15-20 minutes
Baking time: 8-10 minutes

Preheat oven to 450°. Sift together:

**3 cups whole wheat flour (for a lighter biscuit use
half unbleached and half whole wheat flour)**
¾ teaspoon salt
1½ tablespoons baking powder

Cut in with a fork or pastry cutter until mixture resembles fine meal:

1½ cubes butter (¾ cup)

Mix together and stir in:

¾ cup milk
3 eggs, beaten

Shape dough into a ball and roll out on a floured board into a rectangle ½-inch thick. Fold dough into thirds, envelope style, overlapping the ends. Turn dough slightly (about ¼ turn) and roll out lengthwise. Repeat folding and rolling-out process 3 times. Cut dough with biscuit cutter, place biscuits on ungreased cookie sheet, and bake at 450° for 8-10 minutes.

Variation:

Stir in with milk and eggs:

¾-1 cup grated sharp cheddar cheese

Popovers

Makes: 1 dozen

Preparation time: 10 minutes
Baking time: 35 minutes

Preheat oven to 425°. Whisk together:

3 eggs, beaten
1 cup milk
2 tablespoons melted butter
1 teaspoon honey
½ teaspoon salt

Stir in until smooth:

1 cup whole wheat pastry flour

Fill buttered muffin tins or custard cups half-full. Bake in preheated oven at 425° for 15 minutes, then reduce heat to 350° and bake an additional 20 minutes. Do not open the oven door while baking. When done, turn off oven and pierce sides of popovers with a sharp knife to let moisture escape. Allow popovers to dry in oven for 10 minutes. Popovers are best when served immediately.

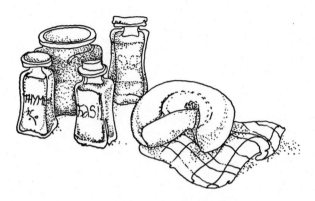

Herb-Cheese Popovers

Makes: 1 dozen

Preparation time: 15 minutes
Baking time: 35-40 minutes

Preheat oven to 425°. Follow the basic popover recipe, eliminating the honey and adding, after stirring in flour:

½ cup grated sharp cheddar cheese
pinch of cayenne
½ teaspoon thyme
¼ teaspoon sage
¼ teaspoon basil
¼ teaspoon paprika

Follow the same baking procedure as with plain popovers, but bake an additional 5 minutes at 350°.

These popovers are not as light as plain popovers—they have more of a muffin consistency.

Gruyère Classique

Serves: 6

A puffed moist cheese bread, to serve with soup, salad, as an appetizer, or with brunch.

Preparation time: 25 minutes
Baking time: 40 minutes

Preheat oven to 400°. Bring to a boil in medium saucepan:

1 cup water
½ cup butter
½ teaspoon salt

Stir in, mixing thoroughly until dough forms a ball in the center:

2 cups whole wheat pastry flour

Remove from heat, allow to cool for a few minutes, then beat in, 2 at a time, mixing thoroughly:

4 large eggs

Set aside to cool. Then add and mix well:

1 cup (packed) grated Gruyère cheese
large pinch of cayenne

On a buttered baking sheet, form dough into a large circle about 8 inches in diameter with a 3-inch hole in the center. Bake at 400° for 10 minutes, then reduce heat to 350° and bake 25 to 30 minutes longer or until ring becomes puffed, dry, and golden brown.

Chappatis

Makes: 30 chappatis

Preparation time: 20-25 minutes
Cooking time: 45 minutes

Combine in medium bowl:
   2 cups whole wheat flour
   1 teaspoon salt

Add gradually until a soft dough is formed:
   ¾-1 cup water

Knead until dough is very pliable. Cover with a damp cloth and let sit for 10-15 minutes. Lightly grease and heat a frying pan, preferably cast-iron. Knead dough once more and break off walnut-size balls. Flatten balls between fingers, dip in flour and roll out evenly and thinly on a floured board. Heat briefly on one side until the edges curl. Turn over and press edges with spatula as bubbles begin to form. The perfect chappati will balloon completely (but don't worry if it doesn't!). Remove from pan and brush lightly with butter. The chappati must be fried quickly or it will turn hard.

Another method of cooking chappatis is to heat lightly on both sides in a frying pan, then place already-fried chappati over medium flame for a few minutes, turning quickly.

Variation:
   For a lighter chappati, use:
   1 cup whole wheat flour
   1 cup unbleached flour

Whole Wheat Cranberry Orange-Nut Bread

Makes: 1 loaf

A good make-ahead holiday bread.

Preparation time: 30 minutes
Baking time: 1 hour and 15 minutes

Preheat oven to 350°. Mix together in medium bowl and let stand:

1½ cups cranberries, coarsely chopped (to save time, chop by using quick on and off motion with blender or food processor)
¾ cup honey

Grate the rind and then juice:

3 medium juice oranges

You should have 3 tablespoons of orange rind. Set rind aside. Peel off white, bitter pith from oranges and coarsely chop oranges. Then mix chopped oranges with orange juice and cranberry-honey mixture. Add:

1 egg, beaten
5 tablespoons melted butter

Sift together:

1¾ cups whole wheat pastry flour
4 teaspoons baking powder
¾ teaspoon baking soda

Add:

3 tablespoons grated orange rind

Combine liquid with dry ingredients. Stir in:

1 cup coarsely chopped walnuts

Spoon mixture into buttered loaf pan. Bake at 350° for 1 hour and 15 minutes. Start checking after 1 hour. Bread is done when a toothpick inserted in the center comes out clean. Cool in the pan or on a wire rack for 10 minutes. Then turn out of the pan and cool completely. Wrap in aluminum foil and refrigerate until the next day (optional).

Please note:

This bread is best served the day after baking.

Applesauce Cornbread

Serves: 8-10

Moist and chewy. Good for breakfast or as a tea bread.

Preparation time: 20 minutes
Baking time: 40 minutes

Preheat oven to 350°. Combine in medium bowl:

2 cups whole wheat pastry flour
1 cup cornmeal
¾ teaspoon salt

Combine in separate bowl:

1 teaspoon baking soda
1 cup buttermilk
⅔ cup honey

Combine wet and dry ingredients. Add:

¾ cup unsweetened applesauce
1 cup raisins

Stir just enough to moisten dry ingredients. Spoon into a well-buttered 8-inch square pan and bake at 350° for 40 minutes.

Pumpkin or Squash Cornbread

Serves: 6-10

Sweet and moist.

Preparation time: 20 minutes
Baking time: 1½ hours

Preheat oven to 350°. Cream in medium bowl:
½ cup soft butter
¾ cup honey

Add and mix well:

2 eggs, beaten
**1½ cups cooked mashed pumpkin or winter squash
(canned works well)**
1 cup milk

Combine in separate bowl:

**1½ cups whole wheat pastry flour or whole wheat
flour**
1 cup cornmeal
1 tablespoon plus 2 teaspoons baking powder
1 teaspoon cinnamon
¼ teaspoon allspice
½ teaspoon salt
⅛ teaspoon powdered ginger

Add dry ingredients to the pumpkin or squash mixture
and mix thoroughly. Spoon mixture into large, buttered
loaf pan, filling it ¾ full*. Bake at 350° for 1½ hours.
(Check after 1 hour to see if done. If top browns too
quickly, cover with aluminum foil.)

Please note:

*Use left-over batter to make muffins. Bake in greased
and floured tins (or tins lined with paper cupcake liners)
at 350° for 15-20 minutes or until done.

Sweet
Cornbread or Muffins

Serves: 6-9

Preparation time: 15 minutes
Baking time: 25 minutes for cornbread, 15-20 minutes for muffins

Preheat oven to 350°. Blend in medium-large bowl and set aside:

½ cup safflower or other light vegetable oil
½ cup honey
2-3 eggs, beaten (3 eggs make the bread more cake-like)

Sift together in medium bowl:

1½ cups whole wheat pastry flour
1 tablespoon baking powder
⅛ teaspoon salt

Mix in with the flour:

1½ cups yellow corn meal

Mix dry ingredients with egg mixture, gradually adding:

1 cup milk

For bread:

Pour into greased and floured 8-inch square pan and sprinkle with:

1 tablespoon poppy seeds

Bake 25 minutes or until done.

For muffins:

Grease muffin tins or use paper cupcake liners. Mixture will make 18-20 average size muffins. Bake at 350° for 15-20 minutes or until done.

Orange-Prune Tea Bread

Makes: 1 loaf

Preparation time: 30-35 minutes
Baking time: 1½ hours
Chilling time: overnight

Preheat oven to 300°. Wash and put through food grinder, using fine blade:

1 medium orange, unpeeled

Boil:

½ cup water

Pour water over:

1 cup(packed) pitted and coarsely chopped dried prunes (use vacuum-packed, pitted variety)

Add to water and let stand:

1½ teaspoons baking soda

Cream together:

1 tablespoon melted butter
⅔ cup honey
1 egg
1 teaspoon vanilla

Sift together:

2½ cups whole wheat pastry flour
1 tablespoon baking powder
½ teaspoon salt

Add dry ingredients to creamed mixture, alternating ground orange with water from the prunes. Stir in prunes and:

1 cup chopped nuts

Spoon mixture into buttered loaf pan. Bake at 300° for 1½ hours or until a toothpick inserted in center comes out clean. Cool in pan for 10 minutes. Remove from pan, cool completely, wrap in aluminum foil and refrigerate overnight.

Quick Oat Bread

Makes: 1 loaf

A sweet, moist bread with a chewy crust.

Preparation time: 15-20 minutes
Baking time: a little over 1 hour

Preheat oven to 350°. Boil for 5 minutes in medium saucepan:

1 cup raisins
1 cup water

Meanwhile, combine in medium bowl:

1 cup oats
1 cup whole wheat pastry flour
1 cup bran
½ teaspoon salt
1 teaspoon cinnamon
¼ teaspoon nutmeg

Mix in separate bowl:

1 cup buttermilk
1 teaspoon baking soda
½ cup honey

Combine wet and dry ingredients, add raisin mixture, and stir only until dry ingredients are moistened. Spoon mixture into buttered loaf pan and bake at 350° for a little over 1 hour. Cool in the pan and then on a cooling rack for 10 minutes. Serve warm or at room temperature.

Spiced Apple Muffins

Makes: 24 muffins

Preparation time: 30 minutes
Baking time: 15 minutes

Preheat oven to 400°. Combine in medium bowl:

1 cup honey
1 cup safflower oil
4 eggs, beaten

Combine in separate bowl:

2½ cups whole wheat pastry flour
2 teaspoons baking powder
½ teaspoon salt
½ cup non-instant milk powder
½ teaspoon allspice
¾ teaspoon nutmeg
2 teaspoons cinnamon

Combine dry and wet ingredients and mix well. Stir in:

2 large apples, peeled, cored, and grated
1½ teaspoons vanilla
¾ cup chopped walnuts
¾ cup raisins

Bake at 400° for 15 minutes in buttered muffin tins.

Carrot Bran Muffins

Makes: 24 muffins

Moist and light.

Preparation time: 20 minutes
Baking time: 20 minutes

Preheat oven to 375°. Combine in medium bowl:

1½ cups whole wheat pastry flour
¾ teaspoon salt
1½ teaspoons baking soda
1½ cups bran
1 teaspoon cinnamon
½ teaspoon nutmeg

Combine in large bowl:

1½ cups milk
2 tablespoons apple cider vinegar
⅓ cup honey
¼ cup molasses
1 cup (packed) grated carrots
2 eggs, beaten
¼ cup safflower oil
¾ cup raisins
½ cup chopped walnuts

Combine wet and dry ingredients. Mix just enough to moisten dry ingredients. Fill buttered muffin tins ⅔ full and bake at 375° for 20 minutes.

There's joy all around us!
Why wait till tomorrow?
   We've only this moment to live.
      A heaven within us
      Is ours for the finding,
         A freedom no riches can give!

Desserts

Rhubarb Fool

Serves: 8-10

A rich yet delicate dessert.

Preparation time: 15-20 minutes
Cooking time: 10-15 minutes
Chilling time: 30 minutes

Steam until soft (about 10-15 minutes):

2 pounds trimmed rhubarb (about 7 large stalks), diced

Place rhubarb in large bowl or serving dish. Add:

¾ cup honey
⅛ teaspoon cinnamon
pinch of nutmeg
pinch of cardamon
pinch of cloves

Mix well, then chill. Whip:

½ pint heavy cream

Blend whipped cream with chilled rhubarb mixture. Garnish with:

fresh mint leaves or strawberries

Cranberry Parfait

Serves: 8-10

A *tangy holiday treat.*

Preparation time: 40 minutes
Chilling time: 3-4 hours

Mix together and set aside:

2 cups ground raw cranberries
1½ cups honey

In a saucepan, mix and let stand for 8 minutes:

1½ cups unsweetened pineapple juice
2 cups freshly squeezed orange juice
11 tablespoons agar flakes

Bring mixture to a boil, then simmer until agar is completely dissolved. Remove from heat and add:

3 tablespoons freshly squeezed lemon juice
⅛ teaspoon salt

Pour mixture into a bowl and place in a sink filled with cold water for 10-15 minutes. Then add cranberry mixture and:

1 cup chopped walnuts
2 cups (packed) halved seedless grapes

Let sit in cold water for another 10 minutes, then fold in:

2 cups whipping cream, stiffly beaten

Spoon mixture into 9-inch by 13-inch dish and place in refrigerator for 3-4 hours. The consistency will be that of a soft mousse. Spoon into parfait glasses and garnish with:

whipped cream, grapes, or sweetened cranberries

Orange-Pineapple Whip

Serves: 7-8

Preparation time: 20-30 minutes
Chilling time: 20-30 minutes

Combine and let soak for 5 minutes:

6 tablespoons agar flakes or powder
2 cups cold water

While the above is soaking, drain:

one 20-ounce can of chunk or crushed unsweetened pineapple (save juice)

After 5 minutes, add to agar mixture:

1 cup hot water

Bring to a boil, then simmer 2-3 minutes, stirring until agar is dissolved. Add:

one 6-ounce can of frozen orange juice concentrate
½ cup honey

Then add:

4 tablespoons freshly squeezed lemon juice plus enough pineapple juice to make 1 cup

Let mixture set for 10 minutes, then gently mix in pineapple. Refrigerate for 20-30 minutes or until set. Whip orange-pineapple jell with electric mixer until frothy (leave some chunks of pineapple unblended). Then whip:

½ pint whipping cream

Fold in whipped cream. Serve right away, or if you like it slightly firmer, refrigerate for 10-15 minutes.

Variation:

> For a fruit salad do not whip jell and omit whipped cream. Serve on a bed of lettuce garnished with:
> **strawberries, kiwi, or other colorful fruit**

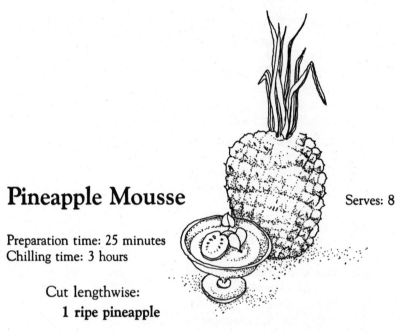

Pineapple Mousse

Serves: 8

Preparation time: 25 minutes
Chilling time: 3 hours

> Cut lengthwise:
> **1 ripe pineapple**

Scoop out fruit from both halves, removing the core. Finely chop the fruit, reserving juice. Mix pineapple with:

> **1½ tablespoons lime juice**
> **½ cup honey**
> **2 cups heavy cream, whipped**

Spoon mixture into an 8-inch square pan. Place in freezer for approximately 3 hours or until slightly firm. (To make this dish ahead of time, freeze the pineapple mixture solid and then remove from freezer 20 minutes before serving to allow it to soften.) Serve garnished with:

> **slices of kiwi and sprigs of fresh mint**

Trailmix Cookies

Makes: 4 dozen

Preparation time: 25-30 minutes
Baking time: 15-20 minutes

Preheat oven to 350°. Blend thoroughly in large bowl:

1½ cups honey or more, to taste (adding more honey
  will make cookies more moist and chewy)
1½ cups safflower oil
2 eggs, beaten

Sift together and add to honey mixture:

4 cups whole wheat pastry flour
2 teaspoons salt
2 tablespoons cinnamon
1 teaspoon baking soda

Stir in:

4 cups rolled oats
5 teaspoons vanilla
½ cup chopped walnuts
½ cup chopped almonds
½ cup chopped cashews
1 cup fine unsweetened coconut
1 cup raisins
1 cup chopped dates
1¾ cups unsweetened carob chips

Drop by large spoonfuls onto lightly greased cookie
sheet. Bake at 350° for 15-20 minutes.

Date-Nut Carob Bars

Makes: 20-24 pieces

Preparation time: 25 minutes
Baking time: 30-35 minutes

Preheat oven to 350°. Combine and let cool:

1¼ cups (packed) chopped dates
1 cup hot water

Beat until creamy in large bowl:

1 cup soft butter
¾ cup honey
2 eggs

Sift together:

1¾ cups whole wheat pastry flour
1½ teaspoons baking soda

Gradually stir flour into butter-honey mixture. Add date mixture and stir in:

1 teaspoon vanilla
¾ cup unsweetened carob chips

Mix well and spread in a buttered 13-inch by 9-inch pan. Top with:

rounded ½ cup unsweetened carob chips
½ cup chopped walnuts or pecans

Bake at 350° for 30-35 minutes or until toothpick inserted in center comes out clean. Cool in pan before cutting. Bars will be somewhat crumbly. Serve with:

whipped cream

Orange-Pineapple Sherbet

Serves: 6

Preparation time: 25-30 minutes
Chilling time: 3 hours

Combine and freeze until firm:

**two 20-ounce cans unsweetened pineapple chunks
(drain chunks well)
5 medium oranges, peeled and cut into chunks
2 tablespoons triple sec (orange liqueur)
1 cup plain yogurt
½ cup honey**

After mixture freezes, cut into chunks and put through a
Champion juicer. Serve immediately or refreeze. Allow
sherbet to soften before serving. Garnish with any
combination of the following:

**mandarin orange sections
sliced kiwi fruit
fresh mint**

Orange-Pumpkin Pudding

Serves: 8-10

Preparation time: 20-25 minutes
Baking time: 50 minutes

Preheat oven to 350°. Combine in large bowl (a whisk works best) and pour into a buttered 2½-quart baking dish:

2½ cups cooked and mashed pumpkin
3 eggs, beaten
scant cup honey
½ teaspoon salt
½ teaspoon allspice
2½ teaspoons cinnamon
¾ teaspoon ground cloves
2 rounded tablespoons grated orange rind
1 cup milk
1 cup half and half
scant cup non-instant powdered milk
1 cup finely chopped walnuts

Bake at 350° for 50 minutes or until knife inserted in center comes out clean. Serve warm or cold with:

whipped cream

Lemon Sponge Custard

Serves: 4-6

Preparation time: 20 minutes
Baking time: 40-50 minutes
Chilling time: 1 hour

Preheat oven to 350°. Cream in medium bowl:

½ cup honey
1½ tablespoons soft butter
2 rounded teaspoons lemon rind
7 egg yolks

Stir in and whisk together:

4 tablespoons whole wheat pastry flour
¼ cup plus 1 tablespoon fresh lemon juice
1 cup milk

Fold in:

7 stiffly beaten egg whites

Pour into custard cups or 8-inch square baking dish and place in a large pan filled with hot water reaching ⅔ up the side of cups or dish. Bake for 40-50 minutes at 350° or until knife inserted in center comes out clean.
Remove custard cups from hot water at once and chill.

Raspberry Torte

Serves: 12

A honey version of Linzertorte.

Preparation time: 40-45 minutes
Baking time: 45-50 minutes
Chilling time: 6 hours

Preheat oven to 350°. Mix together in large bowl:

**1½ cups whole wheat pastry flour
2 teaspoons lemon rind
1½ teaspoons orange rind
⅛ teaspoon salt
1 rounded tablespoon cinnamon
¾ teaspoon ground cloves**

Cut in until mixture resembles coarse meal:

1 cup cold butter

Stir in and mix well:

**⅓ cup plus 2 tablespoons honey
2 egg yolks, beaten
1½ cups ground almonds**

Press ⅔ of the dough into a 9-inch *deep* quiche or tart pan, until dough reaches halfway up the sides. Chill until firm. Mix together and spoon onto chilled crust:

**1½ cups seedless honey raspberry jam
½ cup unsweetened apple sauce**

Using a pastry bag, pipe remaining dough onto jam in lattice pattern. If pastry bag is not available, chill dough very well, roll out between waxed paper, cut into strips and lay lattice-fashion on top of jam. Bake at 350° for 45-50 minutes. Cover with foil if top starts to get brown. Chill thoroughly (6 hours) before serving. Cut in thin wedges and serve with:

unsweetened or lightly sweetened whipped cream

Apple-Custard Tart

Serves: 12

Preparation time: 45-50 minutes
Baking time: 1 hour and 45 minutes
Chilling time: 30-35 minutes

Preheat oven to 400°. To make crust, mix together:
   2 cups whole wheat pastry flour
   ⅛ teaspoon salt
   1 tablespoon grated lemon rind

Cut in and blend until mixture resembles coarse meal:
   1½ cubes cold butter (¾ cup)

Stir in:
   ⅓ cup honey
   1 egg yolk
   2 teaspoons vanilla
   1 cup ground almonds

Press dough into an 11-inch springform pan. Dough
should reach ¾ up the sides. Sprinkle over crust:
   ½ cup ground almonds

Chill until firm (30-35 minutes). In the meantime, soak
and set aside:
   ½ cup currants in
   3½ tablespoons brandy

In a large bowl, combine:
   7 large golden delicious apples, peeled, cored and
      sliced
   1 tablespoon lemon juice
   2 teaspoons cinnamon
   ¼ cup honey

Spoon mixture into chilled crust and bake at 400° for
25 minutes. (Cover with foil after 7 minutes.) Remove
from oven and reduce temperature to 350°.

To make custard, mix together with the soaked currants (including brandy):

4 eggs, beaten
1½ cups half and half
⅓ cup honey
pinch of salt
1 teaspoon vanilla

Pour over apples, evenly distributing currants. Bake at 350° for 1 hour and 15 minutes or until knife inserted in center comes out clean. Cool slightly before removing rim. Serve chilled or at room temperature.

Halva

Makes 16-20 pieces

Preparation time: 25 minutes

Heat together in medium saucepan over medium heat:

1½ cups water
1½ cups milk
1½ cups honey
1½ cups raisins

In a large saucepan, melt:

1½ cubes butter (¾ cup)

Add:

1½ cups almonds or pine nuts, coarsely chopped
1½ cups Farina or cream of wheat

Stir over low heat to brown the nuts and dry the cream of wheat. Then add hot milk mixture a little at a time, stirring until thick. Spoon mixture into buttered 9-inch square pan. Let it set until firm. Cut into pieces.

Flaky Whole Wheat
Pie Crust

Makes: a single 9-inch pie crust

Preparation time: 20-25 minutes

Preheat oven to 400°. Mix in medium or large bowl
(preferably with straight sides):

1½ cups whole wheat pastry flour
¼ teaspoon salt

Blend into mixture with a pastry cutter or two knives
until mixture is crumbly and butter is the size of peas:

½ cup butter

Slowly add, tossing mixture with a fork to distribute
water evenly, *just* until mixture holds together in a ball:

¼ cup cold water (more or less may be needed,
   depending on humidity)

Form mixture into a ball and roll out immediately, or if
the day is warm, refrigerate for 20 minutes and then roll
out. Place dough in a 9-inch pie plate and prick bottom
and sides with a fork. Flute edge. Bake at 400° for 8-10
minutes.

Sweet
Pastry Crust

Makes: a single 9-inch pie crust

Preparation time: 27 minutes

Preheat oven to 425°. Sift together in medium bowl:
1¼ cups whole wheat pastry flour
⅛ teaspoon salt
½ rounded teaspoon baking powder

Add and stir in:
½-1 teaspoon grated lemon rind
2 tablespoons finely ground almonds

Cut in with a pastry blender until mixture resembles coarse meal:
½ cup cold butter

Add and mix well:
2 tablespoons honey
1 tablespoon brandy

Press into 9-inch pie plate. Bake at 425° for 7 minutes. Cover edges with aluminum foil to prevent them from getting too dark. Cool and fill with your favorite filling.

Fruit Shortcake

Serves: 8-9

Preparation time: 45 minutes

Blackberry:

Combine in large saucepan:
2 pounds unsweetened blackberries, fresh or frozen
½ cup honey
4 tablespoons butter
1 cup apple-berry juice

Mix separately:
4 tablespoons cornstarch
½ cup apple-berry juice

Add cornstarch mixture to saucepan and bring to a boil. Cook over low heat until thickened. Remove from heat and add:
1 teaspoon lemon juice

This filling, and the others, will thicken more as they cool.

Blueberry:

Follow the same procedure as above, using the following ingredients:
2 pounds blueberries, fresh or frozen
1½ cups apple-berry juice
½ cup honey
4 tablespoons butter
3½ tablespoons cornstarch
1 teaspoon lemon juice

Cherry:

Follow the same procedure as above, using the following ingredients:

2 pounds dark sweet cherries, fresh or frozen
1½ cups cherry cider
⅓ cup honey
4 tablespoons butter
2 tablespoons cornstarch
1 teaspoon lemon juice

While filling cools, prepare:

Shortcake Biscuits:

Sift together:
1½ cups whole wheat pastry flour
pinch of salt
2 teaspoons baking powder

Stir in:
½ teaspoon grated lemon rind (optional)

Cut in with a knife or pastry cutter, until mixture resembles coarse meal:
4 tablespoons butter

Mix together and add to flour:
½ cup milk
1 tablespoon honey

Stir well. Knead on floured board until dough is smooth—about 30 seconds. Roll dough out to ½-inch thickness. Cut biscuits out with biscuit cutter or a glass. Place biscuits on ungreased cookie sheet and bake at 375° for 10-12 minutes or until golden brown.

To serve, slice biscuits in half, spoon some of the filling on top, cover with the other half of the biscuit, and top with more filling. Delicious with whipped cream or ice cream.

Please note:
These fillings are excellent in pies.

Crunchy Honey Fruit Crisp   Serves: 6

Preparation time: 40-45 minutes
Baking time: 50 minutes

Preheat oven to 350°.

Crust:

Combine and mix well:
   3 tablespoons whole wheat pastry flour
   1½ cups rolled oats
   ½ cup finely chopped pecans
   2 teaspoons cinnamon

Melt together and add to flour mixture:
   6 tablespoons butter
   ½ cup honey

For apple crisp:

Mix together in large bowl:
   12 large cooking apples, peeled, cored and thinly
      sliced
   ⅓ cup honey
   4 teaspoons fresh lemon juice
   2½ teaspoons cinnamon

Spoon apple mixture into 9-inch square buttered baking dish, pressing apples down. (Dish will be very full.) Top with oat mixture. Bake at 350° for 50 minutes. If the topping starts to get too brown, cover with aluminum foil. Crisp is done when apples feel tender when pierced with a fork.

For peach crisp:

Combine:
2 pounds fresh or frozen unsweetened peaches, sliced
¼ teaspoon almond extract
2 tablespoons fresh lemon juice

Heat until melted and mix with peaches:
½ cup honey or, to taste
3 tablespoons butter

Follow baking instructions for apple crisp. Serve at room temperature, topped with:
whipped cream or ice cream

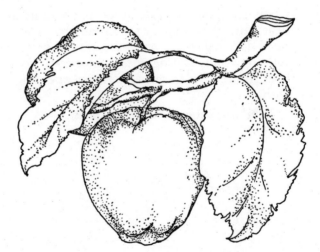

Strawberry Pie

Serves: 6-8

Preparation time: 35 minutes
Chilling time: 1 hour

To make crust, use Sweet Pastry Crust recipe (page 191).
To make filling, arrange points up on bottom of cooled
pastry crust:

1 basket large strawberries

Blend in blender:

2 baskets strawberries
⅓ cup honey
1 tablespoon lemon juice
2½ tablespoons cornstarch

Cook strawberry mixture in medium saucepan over low
heat, stirring constantly for 15 minutes or until mixture
turns dark red. Place pan with strawberry mixture in cold
running water, stirring until almost cool. Pour mixture
over strawberries in pie pan. Refrigerate. Decorate pie
with:

lightly sweetened whipped cream

Strawberry Cake

Serves: 10-12

An elegant strawberry dish.

Preparation time: 1 hour 15 minutes
Baking time: 35 minutes

Preheat oven to 350°. Butter and flour two 8-inch cake pans. Cream in large bowl:

⅔ cup softened butter
1 cup honey
1¼ teaspoons vanilla
4 egg yolks (set aside egg whites at room temperature)

Sift together:

2½ cups whole wheat pastry flour
1 tablespoon baking powder
½ teaspoon salt

Starting and ending with dry ingredients, add dry ingredients to butter mixture, alternating with:

1¼ cups milk

Beat until stiff and fold into batter:

4 egg whites

Pour batter into pans and bake at 350° for 30-35 minutes or until toothpick inserted in center comes out clean. Cool for 5 minutes in pan, then turn out onto cooling racks. When completely cool, slice each layer in half, horizontally, creating four layers. Prepare:

4 cups sliced strawberries (2 small baskets)
6 tablespoons finely chopped almonds, or ¼ cup almonds ground in blender

Whip until stiff:

2 cups whipping cream

Add:

2 tablespoons honey
1 teaspoon vanilla or 1½ teaspoons Grand Marnier or, to taste

To assemble:

Place one layer of cake, cut side up, on cake plate. Spread ¼ of the whipped cream on top. Cover completely with 1 cup strawberries. Sprinkle with 1½ tablespoons almonds. Repeat procedure with remaining layers except for top layer. Cover top layer with whipped cream, placing an extra dollop in the center. Surround with strawberries. Sprinkle with nuts.

Variation:

For added sweetness, spread thinly over the first three layers before topping with whipped cream:

strawberry jam

Orange-Date Cake

Serves: 12

Rich and moist.

Preparation time: 35-40 minutes
Baking time: 1 hour and 15 minutes

Preheat oven to 350°. In a large bowl, combine and soak:

1 cup boiling water
2 cups (packed) chopped dates
1½ teaspoons baking soda

When the water cools, add and set aside:

½ cup freshly squeezed orange juice

Cream together in large bowl:

1 cup butter
1 cup honey
4 eggs, beaten
1 teaspoon vanilla

Combine and add to creamed mixture:

2¼ cups whole wheat pastry flour
1 teaspoon salt
1 teaspoon cinnamon

Stir in soaked dates and:

grated rind of 1½ medium oranges
1 cup chopped walnuts

Spoon into buttered and floured bundt or tube pan. Bake at 350° for 1 hour and 15 minutes or until a toothpick inserted in center comes out clean. Do not frost—serve with:

unsweetened whipped cream

Lazy Daisy Oatmeal Cake

Serves: 8-10

Preparation time: 30 minutes
Baking time: 40-50 minutes

Preheat oven to 350°. Soak in medium bowl for 20 minutes and set aside to cool:

1 cup rolled oats
1¼ cups boiling water

Cream until light:

½ cup butter or margarine
1 cup honey

Beat in:

2 eggs
1 teaspoon vanilla

Set mixture aside. Sift:

1½ cups whole wheat pastry flour

Sift flour again, this time combined with:

1 teaspoon baking soda
½ teaspoon salt
¾ teaspoon cinnamon
¼ teaspoon nutmeg

Stir cooled soaked oats into creamed mixture. Add flour and mix well. Spoon into buttered and floured 8-inch square pan and bake at 350° for 40-50 minutes. Frost with Frosting for Lazy Daisy Oatmeal Cake (opposite page).

Frosting for Lazy Daisy Oatmeal Cake

Preparation time: 10 minutes

Preheat boiler. Combine:

½ cup butter or margarine (room temperature)
1 cup honey
6 tablespoons cream or milk
1½ cups finely flaked unsweetened coconut
⅔ cup chopped nuts

While cake is still hot, spread with frosting and put under preheated broiler until bubbly and tinged with gold. Watch closely, as frosting burns easily. Cool. Serve with:

whipped cream

Upside-Down Plum Cake

Serves: 8

Preparation time: 30-40 minutes
Baking time: 35-40 minutes

Preheat oven to 400°. Combine:

1¼ cups whole wheat pastry flour
1 teaspoon baking powder
pinch of salt

Add and mix well:

⅓ cup honey
3 egg yolks, beaten
1 tablespoon melted butter
¼ cup milk

In a separate bowl, toss:

2 cups halved ripe purple plums
1 tablespoon lemon juice
1 teaspoon grated lemon rind

Melt, thin if necessary with 1 tablespoon water, and press through a sieve:

¼ cup elderberry jelly or jam

Butter an 8-inch or 9-inch square pan. Pour melted jam on the bottom and dot with:

3 tablespoons butter

Drizzle over butter:

¼ cup honey

Drain plums and arrange halves on top of honey, cut side up. Pour batter over plums. Bake at 400° for 35-45 minutes. If the top starts to get too dark, cover with aluminum foil. Cool the cake in pan, then invert onto serving platter. Sprinkle with:

chopped toasted almonds

Serve with:

whipped cream

Apple Cake

Serves: 10-12

Preparation time: 25 minutes
Baking time: 45 minutes - 1 hour

Preheat oven to 350°. Cream in large bowl until fluffy:

3 eggs
1¼ cups honey
1 cup safflower oil
2 teaspoons vanilla
½ teaspoon nutmeg
1 tablespoon cinnamon
1 teaspoon baking soda
¼ teaspoon salt

Add and stir until thoroughly mixed:

2 cups whole wheat pastry flour

Fold in:

4 cups diced apples
1 cup chopped nuts

Spoon mixture into buttered 9-inch by 13-inch pan and bake at 350° for 45 minutes to 1 hour.

Lemon Loaf

Serves: 8-10

Slightly tart.

Preparation time: 25 minutes
Sitting time: 20 minutes
Baking time: 1 hour
Chilling time: 2-3 hours

Preheat oven to 325°. Mix together in large bowl until smooth and creamy:

2 tablespoons butter
½ cup honey
2 large eggs, beaten
½ cup milk

Sift together:

1½ cups whole wheat pastry flour
1 teaspoon baking powder
½ teaspoon salt

Slowly add dry ingredients to creamed mixture, mix well, then add:

1 rounded teaspoon grated lemon rind
2 tablespoons lemon juice
½ cup chopped walnuts

Spoon into standard-size buttered loaf pan and let sit in a warm spot for 20 minutes. Bake at 325°-350° for 1 hour. Cool for 10 minutes in pan, then turn out onto a cooling rack for 10 minutes. Place loaf on a plate. Perforate top by punching holes with a fork. Spoon onto top of loaf a mixture of:

2 tablespoons lemon juice
3 tablespoons honey

Allow loaf to absorb the juice. Chill for 2-3 hours. Slice very thin.

Lemon-Sesame Cake

Serves: 8-9

A uniquely flavored snack cake.

Preparation time: 15-20 minutes
Baking time: 30 minutes

Preheat oven to 350°. Cream together:
> ½ cup butter (room temperature)
> ½ cup tahini
> 2 teaspoons sesame oil
> 1 cup honey
> 3 eggs, beaten
> 1 teaspoon vanilla

Sift together and add to creamed mixture:
> 2¼ cups whole wheat pastry flour
> 1 teaspoon baking powder
> ½ teaspoon baking soda
> ½ teaspoon salt

Stir in:
> 1 tablespoon lemon rind
> ⅓ cup lemon juice
> 3 tablespoons toasted sesame seeds

Spoon mixture into buttered 8-inch or 9-inch square pan. Sprinkle top with:
> 2 tablespoons raw sesame seeds

Bake at 350° for 30 minutes or until toothpick inserted in center comes out clean. Cover with aluminum foil if top starts to brown too quickly. It's best to eat this cake the day it's made.

Carob-Nut Cake

Serves: 10-12

Preparation time: 25 minutes
Baking time: 25-30 minutes

Preheat oven to 350°. Sift together in large bowl:
   1¼ cups whole wheat pastry flour
   ½ cup toasted carob powder
   ½ teaspoon baking powder
   ½ teaspoon baking soda
   ½ teaspoon salt

Cream:
   1 cup butter
   1 cup honey

Add:
   3 eggs, beaten

Fold in dry ingredients, alternating with:
   ½ cup buttermilk

Stir in:
   1 cup chopped nuts
   2 teaspoons vanilla

Pour batter into a buttered 9-inch by 12-inch pan and bake at 350° for 25-30 minutes. Frost with Carob Frosting (opposite page).

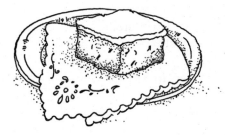

Carob Frosting

Goes well with Carob-Nut Cake.

Preparation time: 10 minutes

In a medium bowl, cream:
5 tablespoons honey
6 tablespoons soft butter

Sift together then gradually add to creamed mixture,
beating with an electric mixer:
⅔ cup non-instant milk powder
½ cup toasted carob powder

Add and beat in:
5 tablespoons cream
¾ teaspoon vanilla

Beat until smooth. Sprinkle frosted cake with:
½ cup finely chopped walnuts

Lemon-
Cream Cheese Chiffon Pie

Serves: 6-8

Preparation time: 45-50 minutes
Chilling time: 2-3 hours

Preheat oven to 375°.

Crust:

To make lemon cookie pie crust, mix thoroughly:
   1½ cups crushed lemon cookie crumbs (we prefer
      the Healthway brand which contains only honey.
      If you use a different brand, you may need to add
      more lemon rind.)
   ¾ teaspoon grated lemon rind
   3 tablespoons butter, melted

Press mixture into pie pan and bake at 375° for
5 minutes, then chill.

Filling:

Combine in blender:
   1 cup cottage cheese
   8 ounces cream cheese, softened
   ¼ cup milk
   ½ cup plus 2 tablespoons honey
   4½ tablespoons lemon juice
   pinch of salt
   2 rounded teaspoons grated lemon rind

Combine, let sit for 5 minutes, then bring to a boil:
   2 teaspoons unflavored gelatin
   ¼ cup cold water

Mix gelatin and cheese mixture together. Whip and fold into above mixture:

½ pint unsweetened heavy whipping cream

Fold in:

1 cup thick plain yogurt

Spoon mixture into chilled crust. Refrigerate for 2-3 hours or until set. Garnish with:

fresh fruit

Sliced kiwi and fresh strawberries are particularly nice.

Pumpkin Cheesecake

Serves: 6-8

Preparation time: 40-45 minutes (including crust)
Baking time: 40 minutes
Cooling time: 1 hour
Chilling time: 30 minutes

Crust:

Preheat oven to 375°. Crush in blender:

3 cups honey ginger snap crumbs (two 5-ounce packages)

Mix with:

½ cup plus 3 tablespoons melted butter
¼ teaspoon powdered ginger
1½ tablespoons honey

Press crumb mixture evenly in the bottom of a 9-inch

springform pan up to ¾ height of pan. Bake crust at 375° for 8-10 minutes.

Filling:

Preheat oven to 400°. Beat until light and fluffy:
   8 ounces cream cheese (room temperature)

Beat in, one at a time:
   2 eggs
   1 egg yolk

Stir in:
   2 cups pumpkin purée
   ½ cup plus 2 tablespoons maple syrup
   1 tablespoon cinnamon
   ½ teaspoon ground ginger
   ¼ teaspoon ground cloves
   ¼ teaspoon allspice
   ¼ teaspoon almond extract (optional)

Pour filling into crust and bake at 400° for 10 minutes. Reduce heat to 325° and bake for 30 more minutes or until center is barely set. Turn off oven and leave in oven for 1 hour. Spread top of cheesecake with a mixture of:
   1½ cups sour cream
   2 tablespoons maple syrup

Chill before serving.

Honey-
Butter Cream Icing

Frosts: two 8-inch layers

Preparation time: 10 minutes

Cream in large bowl:
> 12-14 tablespoons unsalted butter
> ⅔-¾ cup honey

Add:
> pinch of salt
> 3-4 teaspoons vanilla

Sift in:
> 1 cup non-instant milk powder

Add and beat until fluffy:
> 1 tablespoon half and half (or more, if needed for desired consistency)

Variations:

1. Omit half and half and add:
   freshly squeezed lemon or orange juice, and rind

2. Omit honey and use:
   jam or jelly, to taste

Carob Sauce

Makes: 1½ cups

Smooth and creamy.

Preparation time: 10 minutes

Melt in medium saucepan over low heat:
2 cubes butter (½ pound)

Add and whisk until blended:
10 tablespoons raw carob powder
½ cup honey
1 teaspoon cinnamon or more, to taste
2 teaspoons Postum or more, to taste

Heat mixture until it starts to thicken, stirring constantly, then blend in blender until smooth. Serve warm over ice cream or pound cake, and top with chopped walnuts.

If poured into a buttered 8-inch square pan and placed in refrigerator, sauce tends to harden into a fudge-like consistency.

Honey-Nut Sauce

Makes: 3½ cups

Preparation time: 20 minutes

Bring to a boil and boil for 1 minute:

2 cups honey

Add and bring to a boil again:

2 cubes butter, melted (½ pound)

Cook honey-butter mixture at a *very* low rolling boil for 10 minutes (as low as possible). After 10 minutes, remove from heat. Then add and mix well:

2 tablespoons cinnamon
2 teaspoons nutmeg
1½ teaspoons ground cloves
1 teaspoon ginger
1½ cups finely chopped walnuts

Serve as a sauce for crêpes or chilled as a topping for ice cream or yogurt.

Please note:

If overheated, sauce will harden like taffy. If sauce hardens, reheat over very low flame.

If you're seeking freedom
  Seek it on the mountains,
God's sunlight on your shoulders,
   The wind in your hair.

Beverages

Carob Froth

Makes: 4½ cups

Preparation time: 5 minutes

Combine in blender:
**4 cups milk
6 rounded tablespoons raw carob powder
4 tablespoons honey
1 teaspoon cinnamon
1 teaspoon vanilla**

Spicy Carob Milk

Makes: 3½ cups

Delicious cold or hot—almost a meal in itself.

Preparation time: 5-10 minutes

Combine in blender:
**3 cups milk
1½ teaspoons molasses
1½ tablespoons honey
1 tablespoon toasted carob powder
½ teaspoon vanilla
¼ teaspoon powdered cardamon
½ teaspoon cinnamon
pinch of nutmeg
pinch of Postum**

Variation:
When served cold, blend in:
1 banana

Lhassi

Preparation time: 8 minutes

This sweet, refreshing drink is simple to make. Traditionally served with Indian food, it is the only recipe in this book which calls for sugar. The charm of the drink is the subtle balance of sweet and sour, and honey is too heavy a sweetener to work well. It is possible to use honey—you'll just have a somewhat different drink.

The recipe below is a guideline only. The proportions will vary, depending on how thick or tart the yogurt is. Adjust them to suit your taste. The drink, however, should be thin.

Blend in blender:

1 cup yogurt
3 cups water
⅓ cup sugar
⅛ rounded teaspoon cardamon
1 tablespoon lemon juice
1 tablespoon pure undiluted rosewater or more, to
    taste (rosewater is inexpensive, and you can buy
    it from a pharmacy. Be sure to specify
    undiluted.)

Ginger Tea

Makes: 4-5 cups

A wonderful winter drink.

Preparation time: 10 minutes

Bring to a boil and boil for 5 minutes:
1 quart water
½ cup milk
¼ cup honey or more, to taste
1 teaspoon powdered ginger or more, to taste

Spicy
Mandarin Orange Tea

Makes: 7 cups

A spicy aromatic blend.

Preparation time: 10 minutes

Steep for 5 minutes:
1 quart boiling water
5 bags mandarin orange spice tea

Remove tea bags and add:
1 teaspoon vanilla
1 teaspoon cinnamon
1 teaspoon allspice
1 teaspoon nutmeg

Add and stir in:
12 ounces undiluted unsweetened orange juice concentrate
16 ounces undiluted unsweetened apple juice concentrate

Adjust water and spices to taste, if necessary. Serve hot or cold with:
cinnamon stick
slice of orange or lemon

Red Zinger Apple Punch

Makes: 3 quarts

Preparation time: 5-8 minutes

Steep for 5 minutes:
   8 cups boiling water
   8 bags Red Zinger tea

Remove tea bags and stir in:
   ½ cup honey

Then add:
   1 quart unsweetened apple juice
   juice and pulp of 2 limes (do not strain)

Garnish with:
   fresh mint leaves

Serve hot or cold.

Apple-Red Zinger Iced Tea

Makes: 2 quarts

Preparation time: 15 minutes
Chilling time: 1 to 2 hours

Let steep for 5 minutes:
   4 cups boiling water
   8 bags Red Zinger tea

Remove tea bags, pour tea into a 2½-quart pitcher, and stir in:
   2 tablespoons honey

When honey is completely dissolved, add:

3 cups apple juice
1 cup cold water
2 teaspoons lime juice

Refrigerate. Serve over ice and garnish with:

slice of lemon or lime

North African
Iced Mint Tea

Makes: 1 quart

A favorite on a warm summer evening.

Preparation time: 15 minutes
Chilling time: 1-2 hours

Let steep for 5 minutes:

4 cups boiling water
6 peppermint tea bags

Remove tea bags and add:

6 tablespoons honey (¼ cup plus 2 tablespoons)
1 tablespoon plus 2 teaspoons fresh lime juice
(1-2 limes)

Refrigerate for 1-2 hours. Serve over ice and garnish with:

slice of lemon or lime

To cool more quickly, use only 3 cups of boiling water and add 1 cup of cold water before adding ice.

Tropical Cooler

Makes: 2½ cups

Preparation time: 5-10 minutes

Combine in blender:
    6 tablespoons papaya juice concentrate (3 ounces)
    6 tablespoons pineapple-coconut juice (3 ounces)
    ¾ cup freshly squeezed orange juice (2-3 oranges)
    2 ice cubes
    1¼ cups water or, to taste

Serve over ice. Garnish with:
    sprig of mint

Variation:
    Before blending, add:
        1 scoop of honey-vanilla ice cream

Honey-Lemonade

Makes: 1½ quarts

Preparation time: 10-15 minutes
Chilling time: 1-2 hours

Heat in small pan over medium heat until honey
dissolves:

1 cup water
¼ cup honey

Mix together in pitcher:

honey-water mixture
4 cups cold water
¾ cup freshly squeezed lemon juice (3-4 lemons)

Add:

5 strips lemon rind
1 medium orange, thinly sliced

Refrigerate for 1-2 hours. Remove lemon rind and orange
slices before serving.

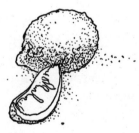

The secret of laughter lies in the laughing,
Not in the search for joy:
It's a swallow winging on the wind;
It's innocence in a boy.

This & That

A Few Breakfast Ideas

Millet Pudding

Serves: 8

Preparation time: 40-45 minutes

In a large saucepan, sauté over medium heat for a few minutes until millet begins to toast (about 8 minutes), stirring frequently:

2 tablespoons safflower oil
2 tablespoons butter
2 cups millet

Add and bring to a boil:

5 cups water
2 sticks cinnamon
16 whole cloves
¼ teaspoon ground cardamon
½ teaspoon ground coriander
1½ cups (packed) chopped dates or date pieces
½ cup honey (optional)

Reduce heat, cover and simmer for 25 minutes or until water is absorbed. Add and stir in:

4 cups milk

Continue simmering very gently, stirring frequently until milk is absorbed and mixture is thick and creamy (about 20-30 minutes). Serve hot or cold. If desired add cream or milk.

Oatmeal Supreme

Serves: 8

Preparation time: 20 minutes

Combine in large saucepan and bring to a boil:
5 cups water
1½ teaspoons coriander
⅛ teaspoon ground cloves
¼ teaspoon powdered ginger
¾ teaspoon cinnamon

After water and spices come to a boil, add:
3¼ cups rolled oats
½ cup raw sunflower seeds
2 cups milk
2 cups grated apples
1 teaspoon vanilla
1 tablespoon fresh lemon juice

Cook over low heat until thickened. Top with honey
and additional milk if desired.

Variation:
To every 2 cups of water add and purée in blender:
1 banana

Cook oatmeal in this "banana milk".

Apple Muesli

Preparation time: 35 minutes
Soaking time: overnight

Soak in large bowl for 2-3 hours:
¾ cup rolled oats
1½ cups water

Drain off excess water. Add:
juice of 3 large lemons
¼ cup honey
½ cup cream

Then quickly add, stirring immediately to prevent apples from browning:
8 large apples, peeled, cored and grated (red delicious work best)

Stir mixture thoroughly and refrigerate overnight. Before serving, stir in:
4 large ripe bananas, mashed with a fork

Add:
1 teaspoon cinnamon
¼ teaspoon nutmeg
¼ teaspoon coriander
1 teaspoon lemon rind
1 cup ground almonds or more, to taste
raisins or currants, to taste

Variations:
1. Serve with:
sliced bananas

2. For a grainier mixture, increase the proportion of oats.

Appetizers and Snacks

Cheese Crackers

Makes: 20-25

Crisp and flaky.

Preparation time: 15 minutes
Baking time: 12 minutes

Preheat oven to 475°. Mix together in medium bowl:
  4 tablespoons soft butter
  ¼ pound sharp cheddar cheese, grated
  1 teaspoon tamari

Stir in and work with fingers until well blended:
  ¾ cup whole wheat pastry flour
  ¼ teaspoon salt
  pinch of onion powder
  pinch of chile powder
  pinch of curry powder

Press mixture onto an oiled cookie sheet ¼-inch thick. Prick with a fork and cut into squares. Bake at 475° for 12 minutes.

Tofu-Chile Cheese Squares

Serves: 5-6

Rich and cheesy.

Preparation time: 30 minutes
Baking time: 30-35 minutes

Preheat oven to 350°. In blender, purée in 2 or 3 batches until smooth and pour into large bowl:

3 eggs
¾ pound tofu
½ teaspoon salt

Stir in:

1 pound cheddar cheese, grated
one 7-ounce can green Ortega chiles, chopped

Spread mixture evenly in a buttered 8-inch square pan and sprinkle with:

1½ tablespoons finely grated fresh Parmesan cheese
paprika

Bake at 350° for 30-35 minutes. Can be a main dish or appetizer.

Mexican Cheese Melts

Serves: 6-8

A do-ahead time-saver.

Preparation time: 10 minutes

Mix together in medium bowl:

4 ounces sharp cheddar cheese, grated
4 ounces mozzarella cheese, grated
1 small can chopped Ortega green chiles
1 large clove garlic, crushed
1 cup mayonnaise

Spread mixture on sliced sour dough bread. Place slices
on cookie sheet and freeze until firm. When frozen, stack
slices and store in plastic bag in freezer. Take out as
needed. Do not defrost. Bake at 325° until cheese is
melted. Excellent for brunches, lunches, and, on cocktail
rounds, as an appetizer.

English Muffin Melts

Serves: 6-8

Preparation time: 15 minutes

Preheat oven to 400°. Mix together in medium bowl:

one 4-ounce can chopped black olives, drained
2 tablespoons finely chopped onion
1 teaspoon curry powder
½ teaspoon garlic powder
1 cup grated sharp cheddar cheese
2 tablespoons mayonnaise

Spread on English muffins and bake at 400° until cheese
melts. Cut muffins into quarters and serve as appetizers.
Mixture can also be spread on crackers and served cold.

Marinated Mushrooms   Makes: 1½ cups, drained

Preparation time: 12-15 minutes
Marinating time: 24 hours

Combine in small bowl and whisk together:
  ½ cup apple cider vinegar
  ½ cup olive oil
  2 teaspoons basil
  2 teaspoons marjoram
  2 teaspoons yellow mustard seeds
  1 teaspoon onion salt
  ¼ teaspoon garlic powder
  2-3 dashes Worcestershire sauce
  pinch of cayenne

Pour mixture over:
  3 cups (packed) small button mushrooms or thickly
    sliced larger mushrooms (approximately ½
    pound)

Refrigerate mushrooms for 24 hours, stirring occasionally.
Drain and serve as an appetizer, or leave in marinade and
serve on crisp lettuce leaves as a salad.

Marinated Tofu

Makes: 5 cups, drained

Preparation time: 20-25 minutes
Marinating time: overnight

Combine in blender:
   1 cup lemon juice
   1 cup tamari
   1½ cups sesame oil
   1 teaspoon grated fresh ginger
   2 teaspoons basil
   6 large cloves garlic, peeled
   1 teaspoon apple cider vinegar

Pour mixture over:
   1½ pounds firm tofu, cut into small cubes

Marinate tofu overnight in refrigerator, stirring
occasionally. Serve as a main dish, side dish, or as an
appetizer. The marinade can be re-used for another batch
of tofu.

Herbed Croutons

Makes: 2½ cups

Preparation time: 30 minutes

Crush in mortar:
1 tablespoon thyme
1 teaspoon basil
1 teaspoon paprika
½ teaspoon oregano
2 rounded tablespoons minced fresh parsley
1 teaspoon onion powder
3 large cloves garlic

Combine herb mixture with:
1 cube butter, melted (¼ pound)

Brush mixture onto both sides of:
9-10 slices whole wheat bread

Cut bread into cubes and toast in a dry skillet for 10-15 minutes, or until crisp and browned. Watch closely so that croutons don't burn. They can be frozen for later use.

Raja Popcorn

Makes: 4 quarts

Great tasting and good for you.

Preparation time: 12 minutes

> Pop:
> **big bowl of popcorn (about 4 quarts)**
>
> Add and mix well:
> **4-6 tablespoons melted butter or more, to taste**
>
> Sprinkle popcorn with a mixture of:
> **¾ cup nutritional yeast**
> **2-3 teaspoons curry powder**
>
> Add:
> **salt, to taste**

Index

---

*Joy will come to anyone
Whose soul has learned to fly!*

NOTES